I0485225

Dundas Ontario in Colour Photos Book 2, Saving Our History One Photo at a Time

Photography
by Barbara Raué
2012

Series Name:
Cruising Ontario

Book 54: Dundas in Colour Book 2

Cover photo: South Street "Wedding Cake House"

Series Name: Cruising Ontario
Saving Our History One Photo at a Time

Photos now in full colour
Check the Appendixes in the back of each book for
descriptions of architectural terms and building styles

Book 33: Southampton
Book 34: Jarvis
Book 35: Hagersville
Book 37: Simcoe
Book 38: Cambridge Part 1 – Galt Book 1
Book 39: Cambridge Part 1 – Galt Book 2
Book 40: Cambridge Part 2 – Preston
Book 41: Cambridge Part 3 – Hespeler
Book 42: Kitchener Book 1
Book 43: Kitchener Book 2
Book 46: Shelburne
Book 47: Alton, Mono and Caledon
Book 48: London in Colour
Book 50: Orangeville Beginnings in Colour
Book 51: Orangeville on Broadway in Colour
Book 52: Orangeville Book 3 in Colour
Book 53: Dundas in Colour Book 1
Book 54: Dundas in Colour Book 2
Book 55: Dundas in Colour Book 3
Book 56: Stratford
Book 57: Hanover

Other Books by Barbara Raue

Coins of Gold

Arrows, Indians and Love

The Life and Times of Barbara
Volume 1: Inventions That Have Enhanced My Life
Volume 2: Entertainment That I Have Enjoyed
Volume 3: East Coast Trips
Volume 4: Olympics Have Always Intrigued Me
Volume 5: Wonders of the World
Volume 6: Caribbean Cruises We Have Enjoyed
Volume 7: Animals
Volume 8: Storms and Other Major Disasters in My Lifetime
Volume 9: Wars, Terrorist Attacks and Major Disasters

The Cromwell Family Book

Visit Barbara's website to view all of her books
http://barbararaue.ericraue.com

Dundas, Ontario

Dundas was originally known as Cootes Paradise, named after Captain Cootes of the Kings Royal 8th Regiment and was incorporated as a town in 1847. Its tree lined streets, heritage homes and picturesque downtown reflect the nostalgic quality of the past. Businesses, found in renovated Victorian buildings, were mostly built of limestone or brick after a fire in 1881 destroyed original wooden buildings. Downtown consists of two blocks along King Street West with specialty stores. Fran White, the owner of Heirlooms Bridal Saloon, says the building used to be Hugh Walker's Hardware Store built in 1883. They renovated the building in 1987 but kept the original 14-foot ceilings, wooden floors, long counter and sliding rail ladder. Terraware is a hemp shop where all products are environmentally friendly. Mickey McGuire's Cheese Shop offers a wide selection of cheeses from around the world. Inside the Ukrainian Store there are pirogues, traditional meats and delicious biscuits. The arts helped shape the destiny of Dundas which is home to many artists who have achieved international fame. Off the main street is the Dundas Valley School of Art set in an 1830s one time munitions factory on Ogilvie Street. Learn more Dundas history at the Dundas Museum and Archives on Park Street West. Drive slowly down Victoria Avenue to admire gorgeous stately historical homes. Taylor's Tearoom is a great place to have lunch or afternoon tea. The Keeping Room is a fabulous kitchen shop.

Index

Sydenham Street

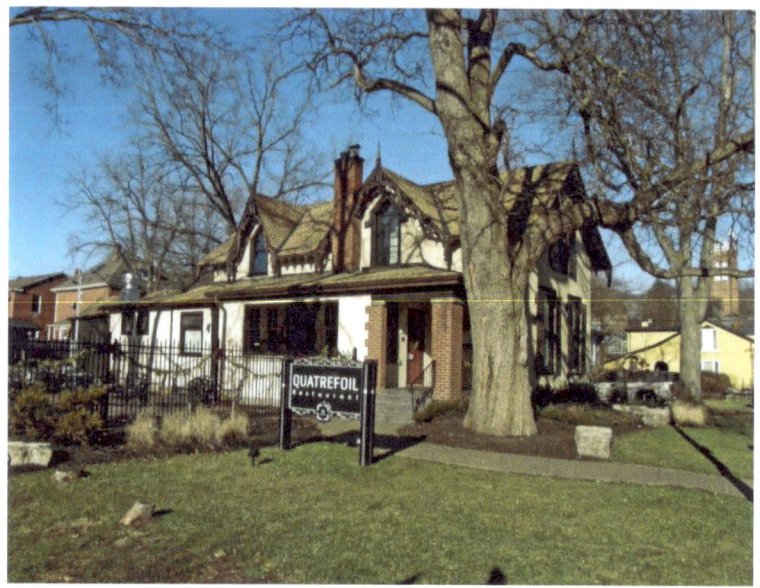

Quatrefoil Restaurant – Gothic Revival – gingerbread trim on gables

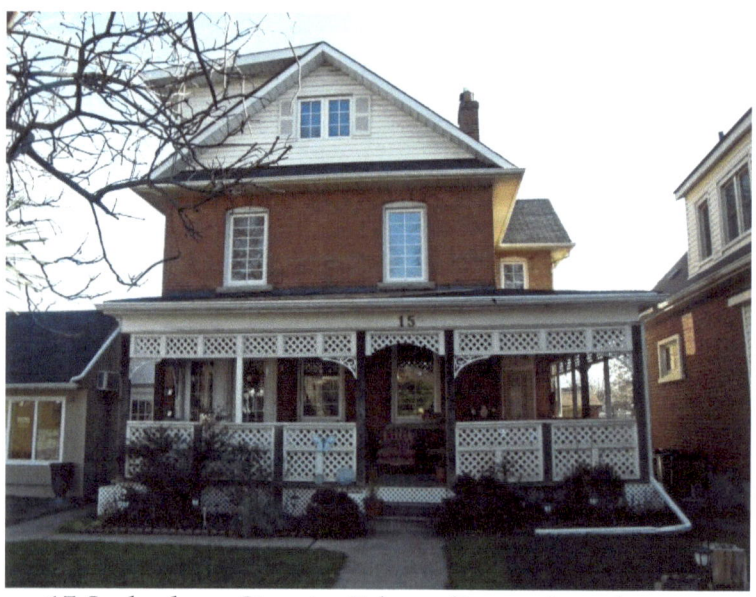

15 Sydenham Street – Edwardian style – dormer

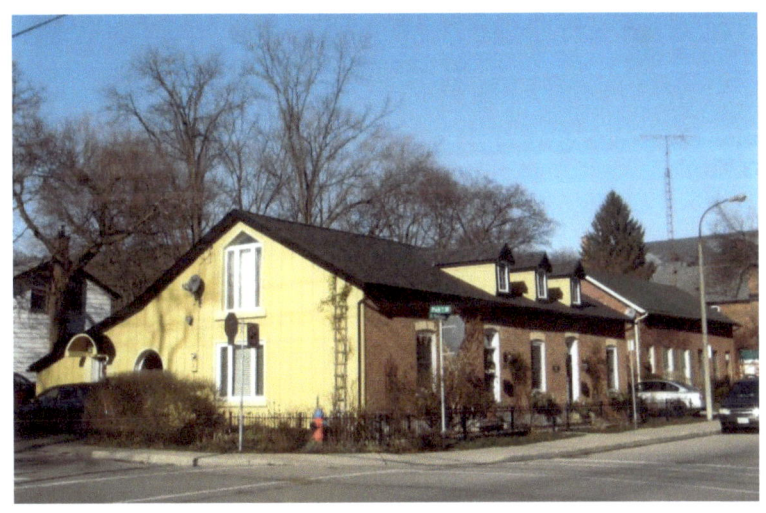

Blacksmith Cottage circa 1859

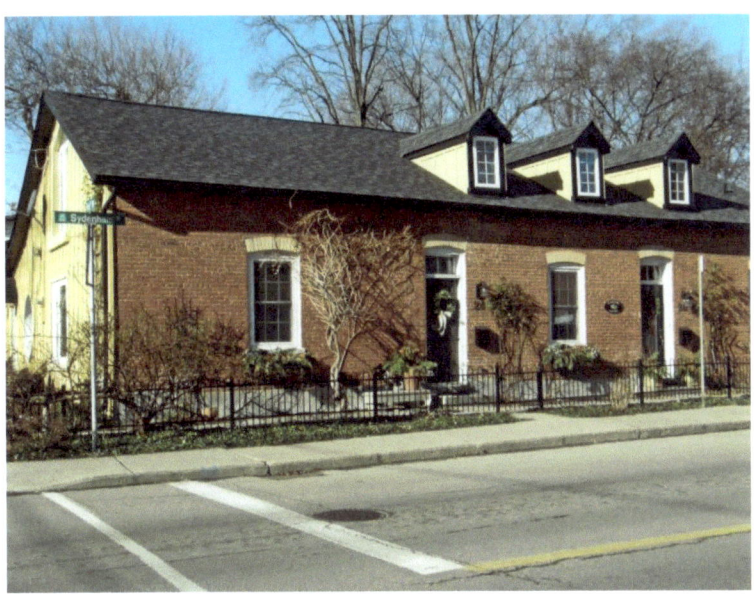

Dormers in the attic

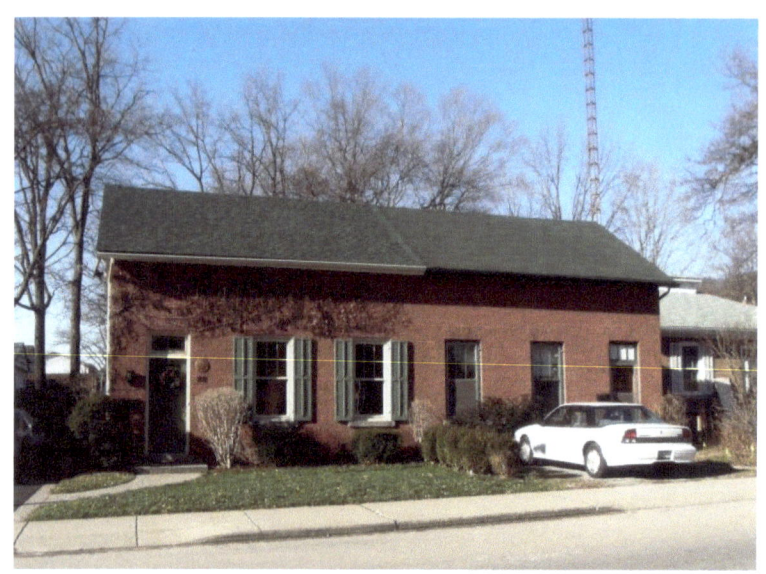

30 Sydenham Street – circa 1870s

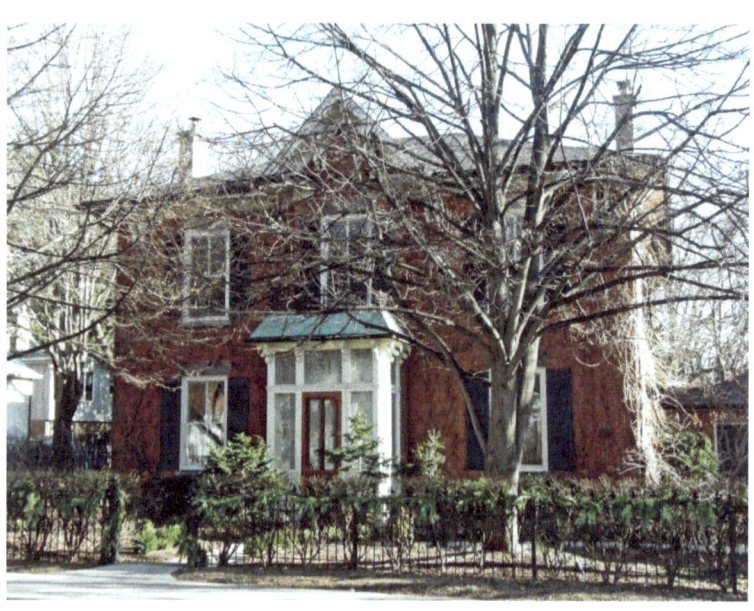

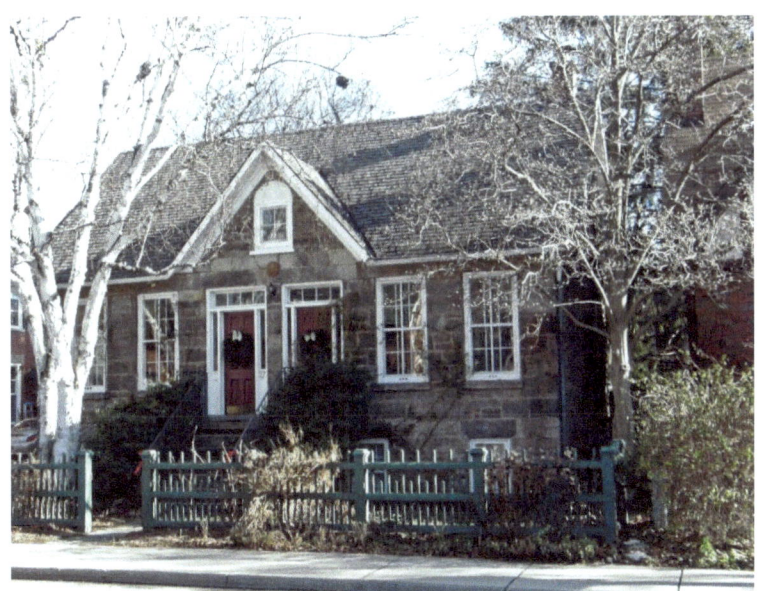

27 Sydenham Street – Gothic Cottage - circa 1850s

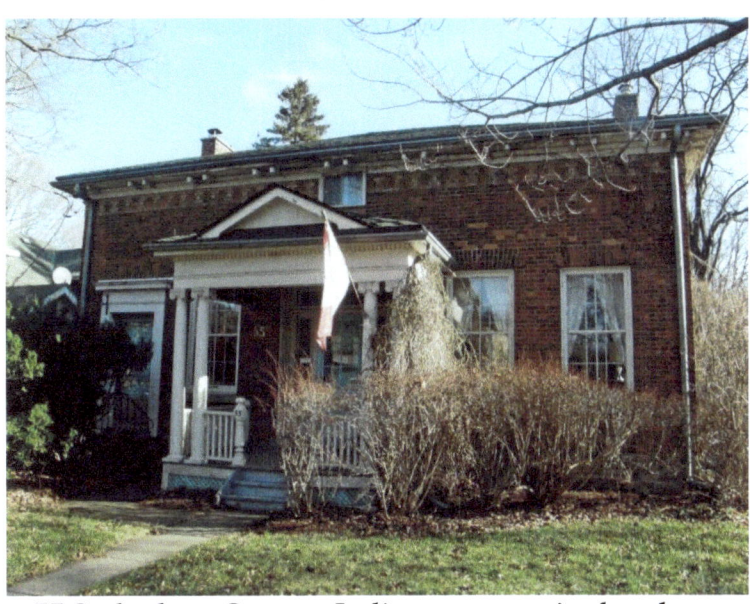

55 Sydenham Street – Italianate – cornice brackets, dichromatic brickwork

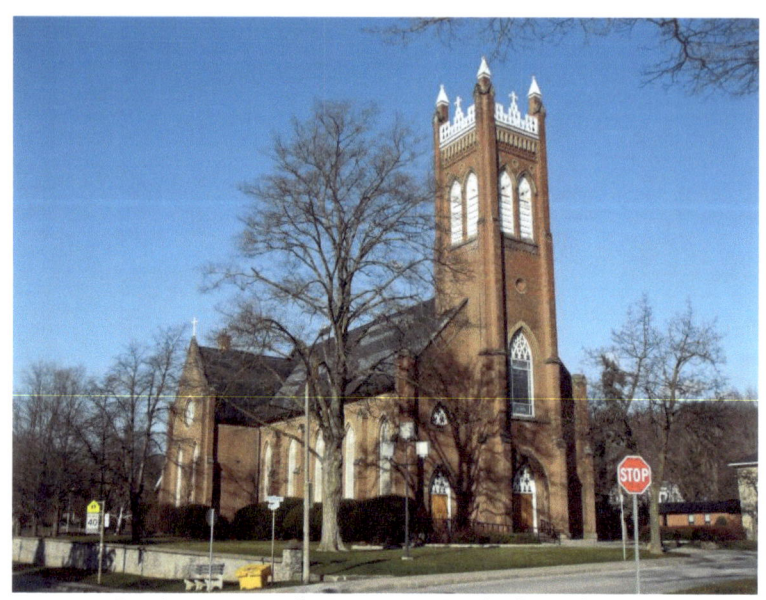

St. Augustine's Roman Catholic Church
Sydenham Street

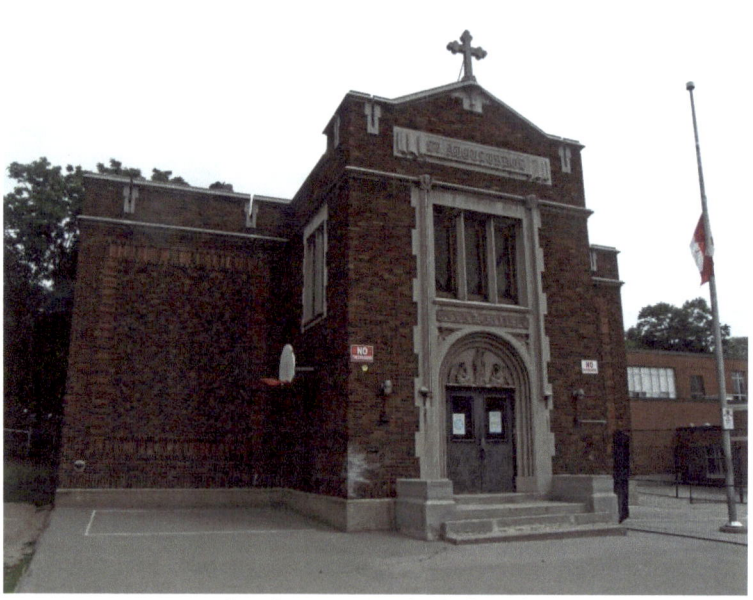

St. Augustine's School

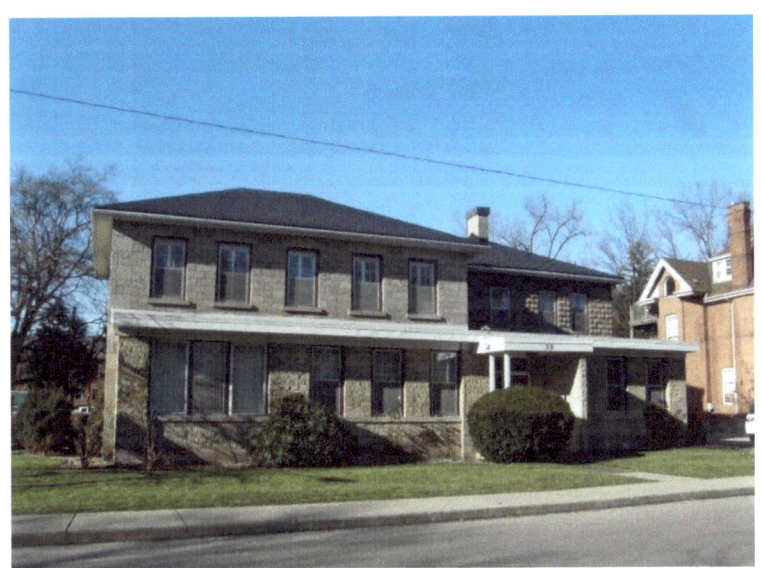

58 Sydenham Street

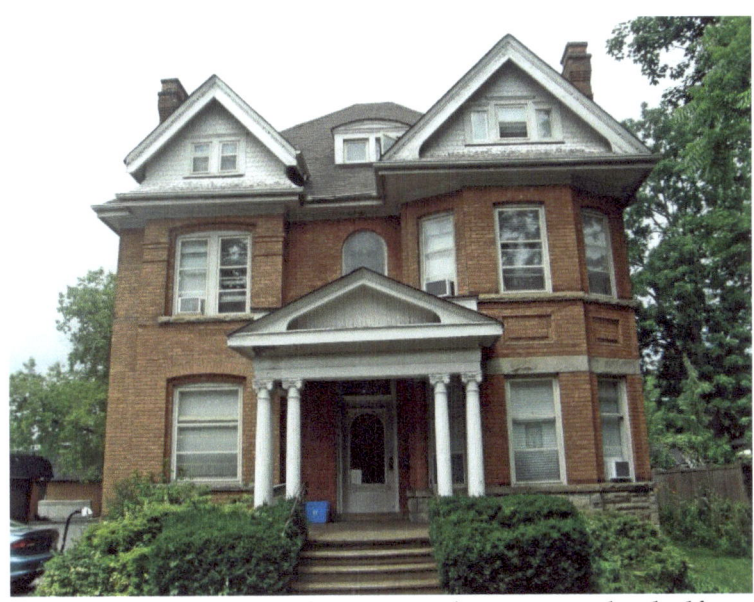

60 Sydenham Street – Italianate with a two-and-a-half storey
tower-like bay, pediment above doorway

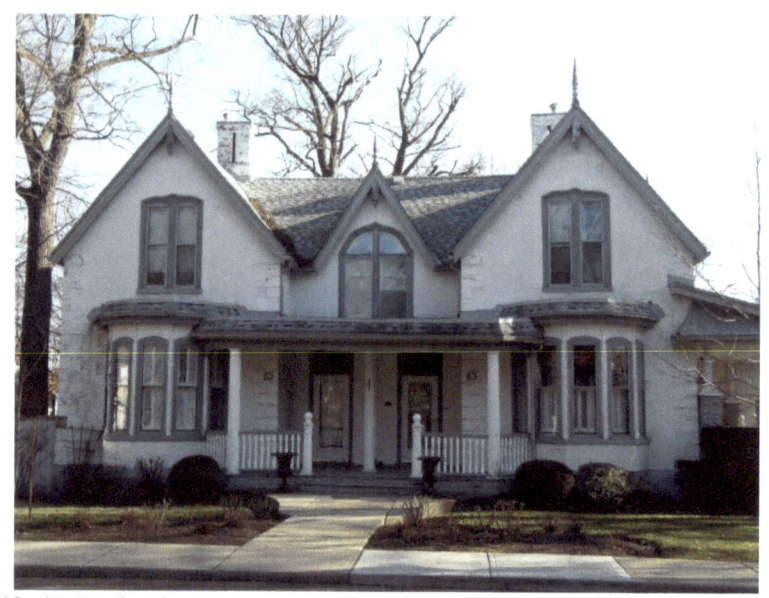

63-65 Sydenham Street – three gable Gothic Revival Style
Finials on gables

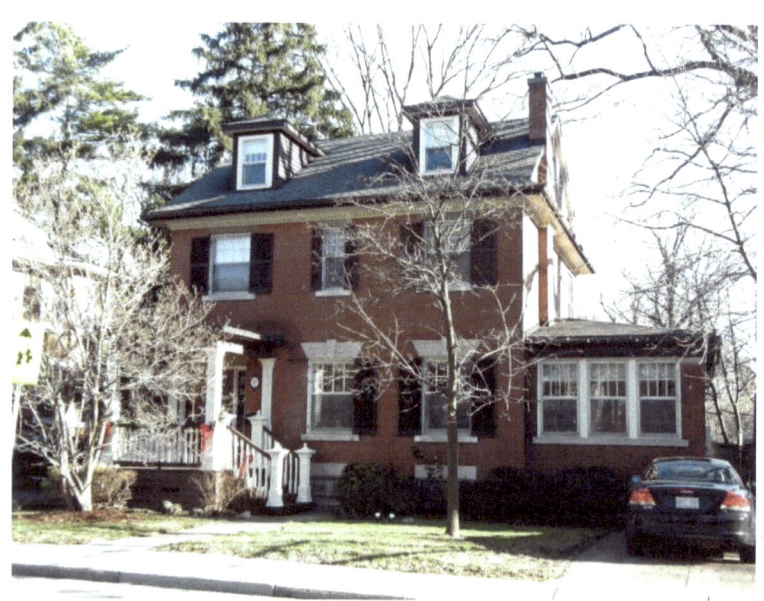

67 Sydenham Street – dormers in attic

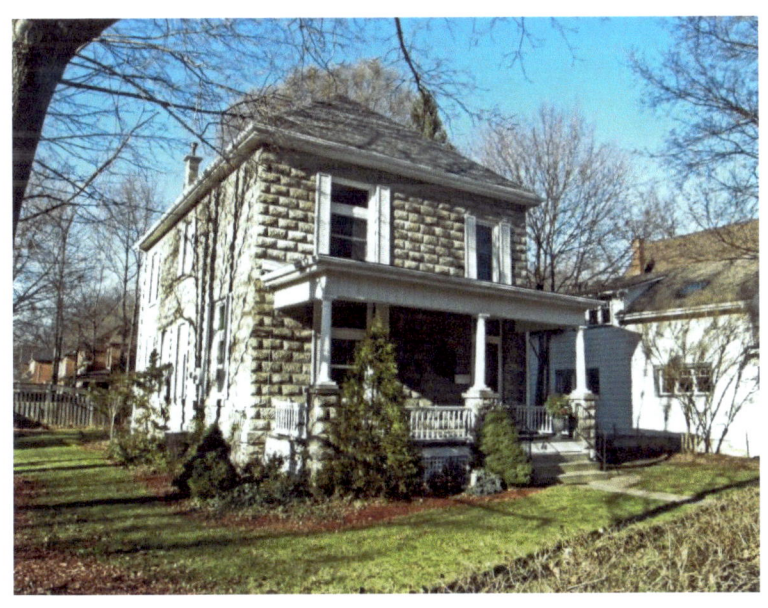

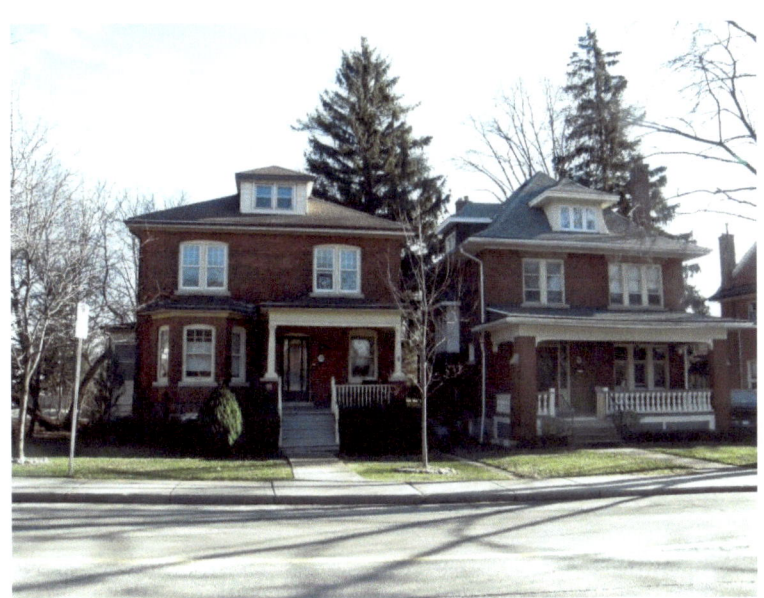

71 and 73 Sydenham Street – Italianate – dormers in attics

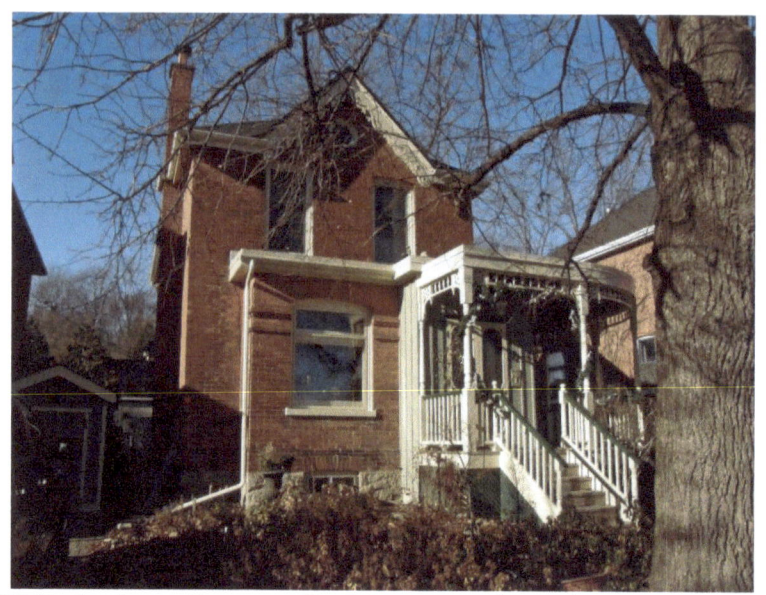

72 Sydenham Street – Gothic – vergeboard trim on gable

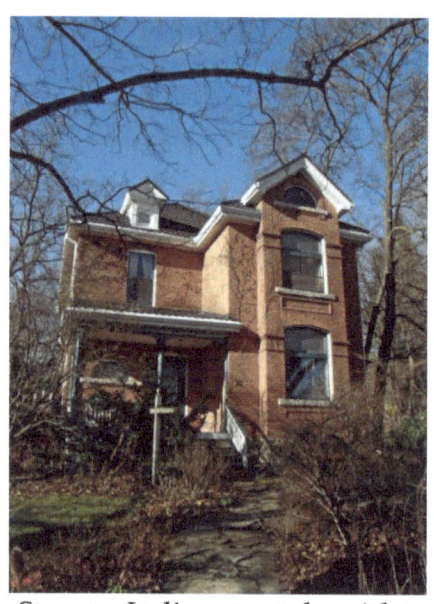

76 Sydenham Street – Italianate style with two-and-a-half storey tower-like bay, dormer in attic

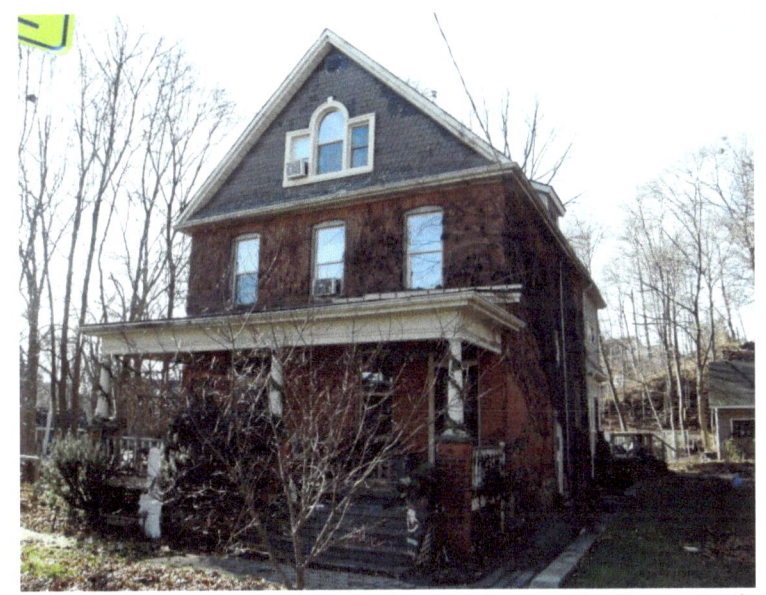

82 Sydenham Street – Edwardian style – palladian window

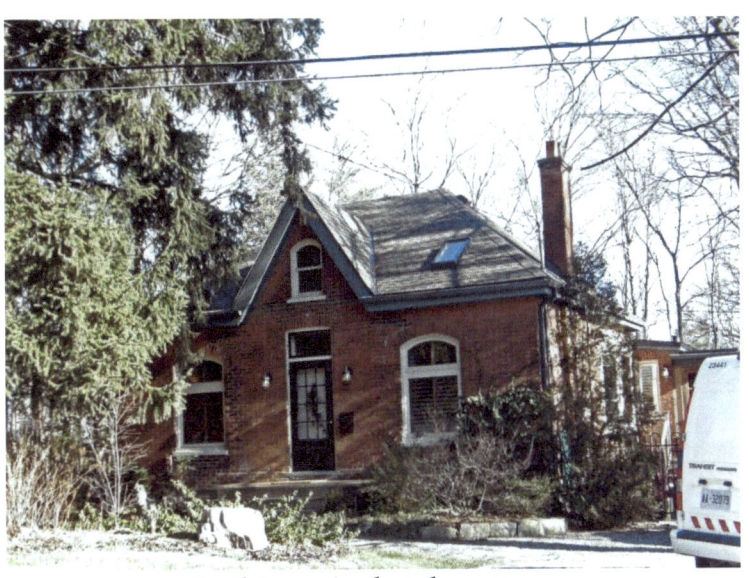

Gothic revival style cottage

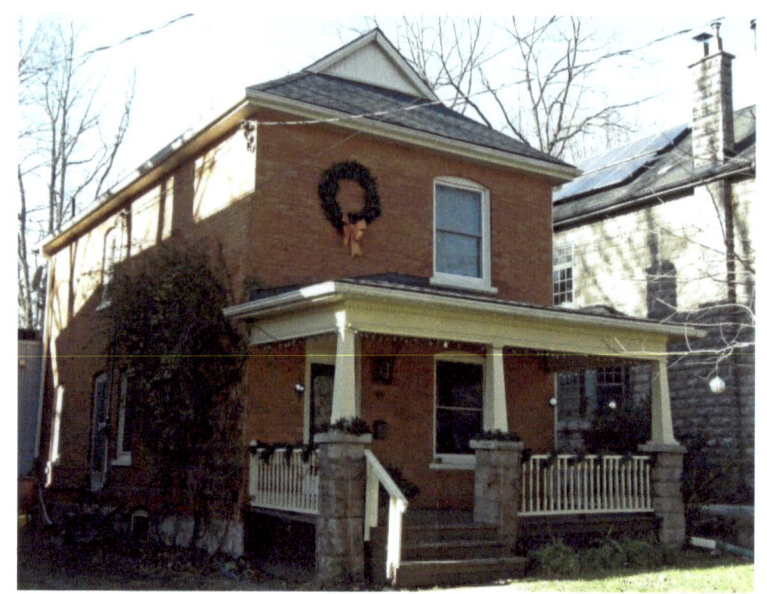

92 Sydenham Street – Italianate style

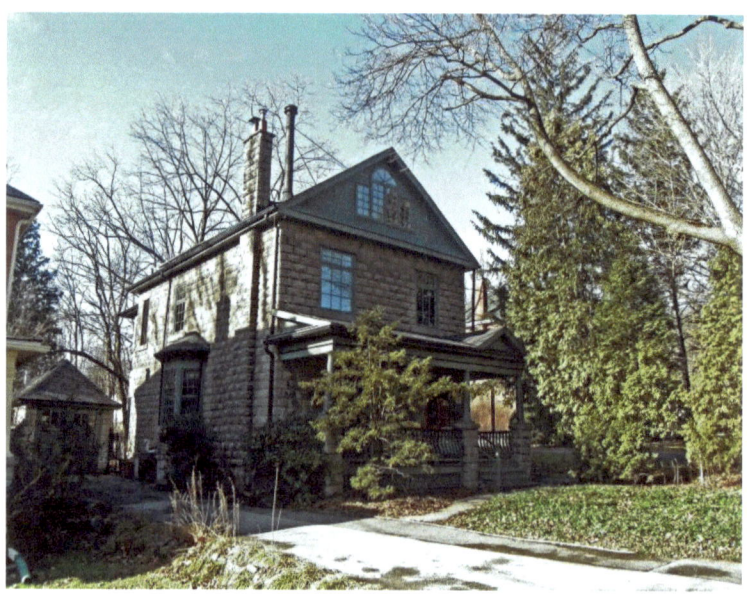

Cement block house – cheaper to construct

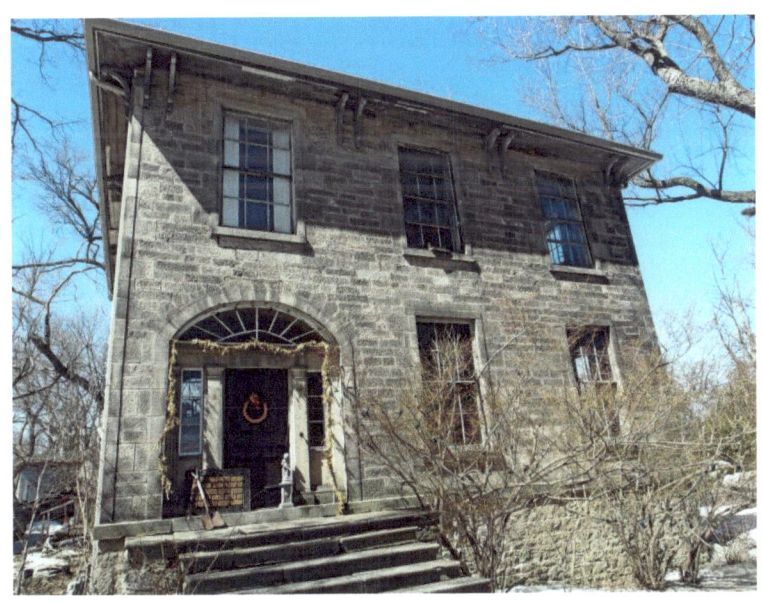

295 Brock Road – Italianate – paired cornice brackets

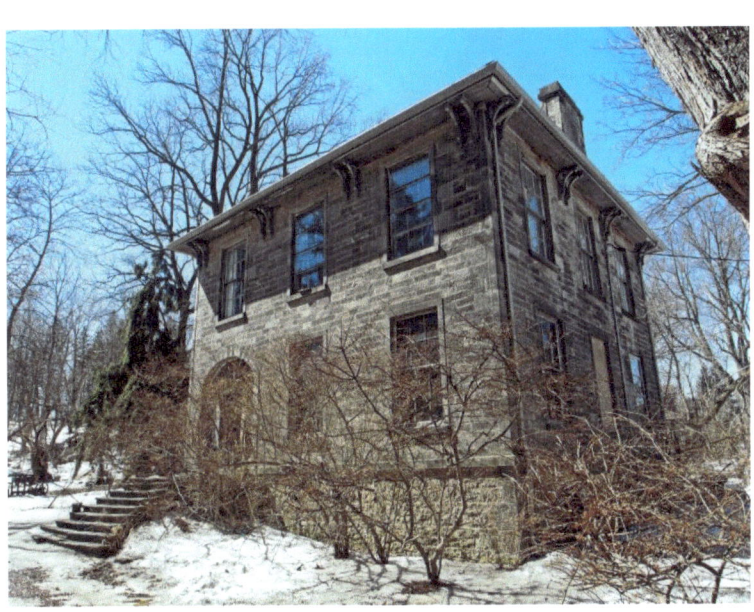

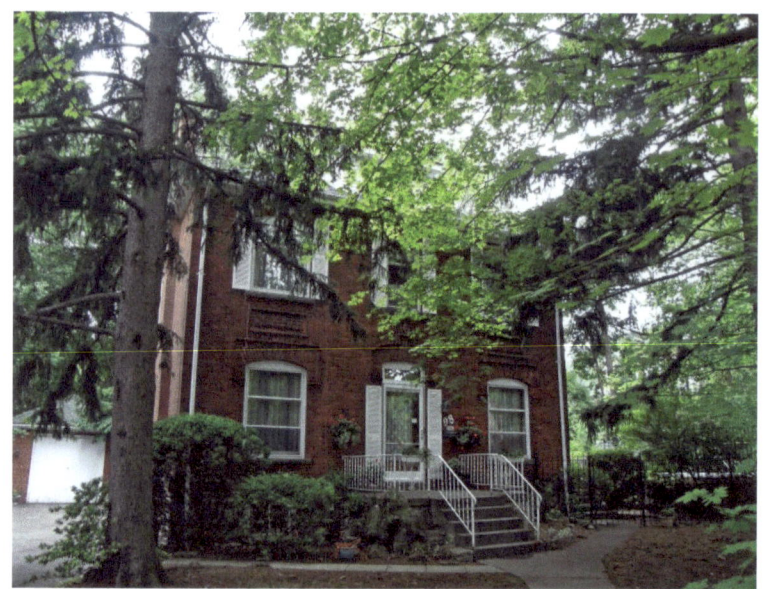

98 Sydenham Street – a beauty hidden among the trees

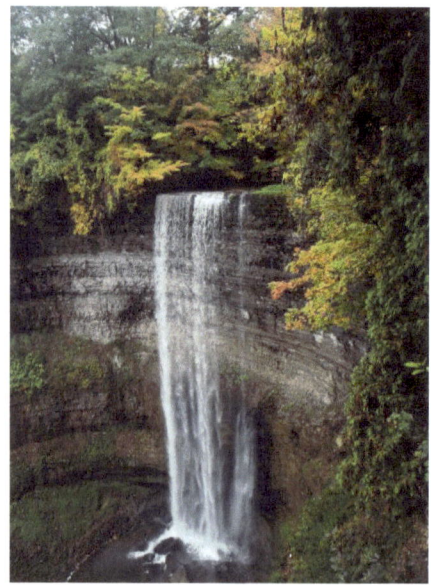

Tew's Falls

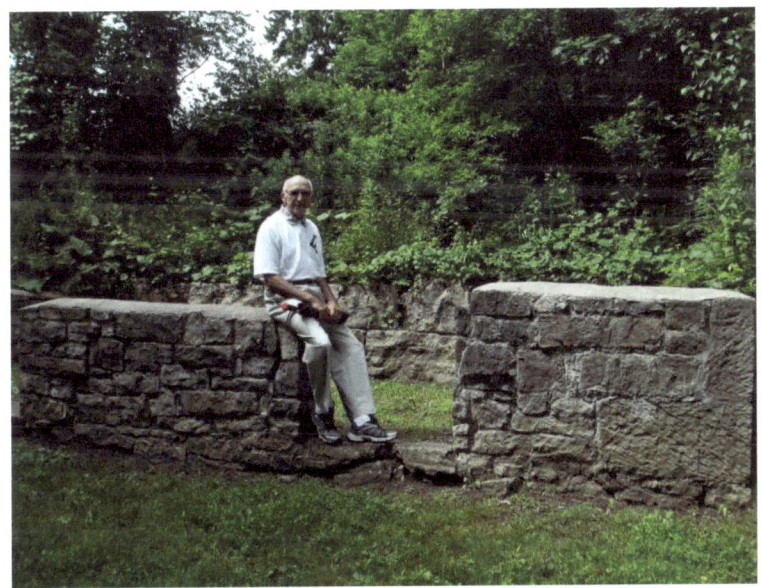

Remnants of an 1840s Mercantile Block at Bullock's Corners consisting of a general store, shoemaker shop, harness shop, flour and feed store, and a public hall

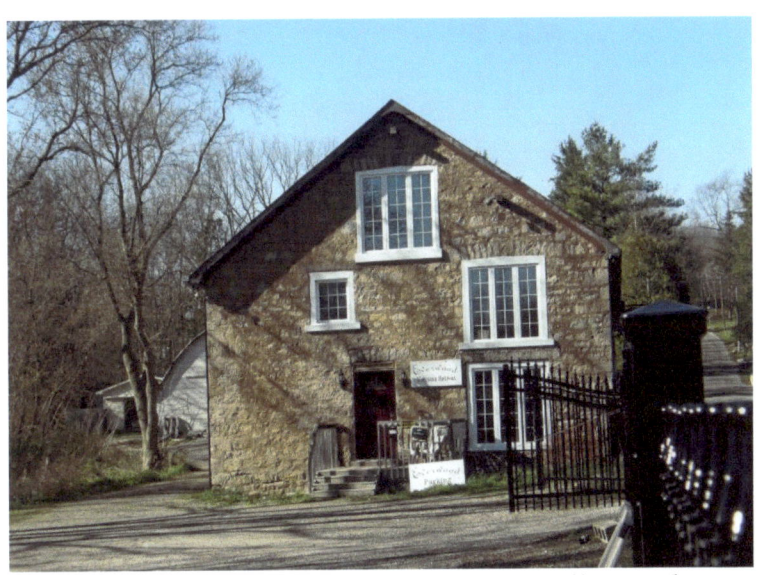

Old stone building on Webster's Falls Road

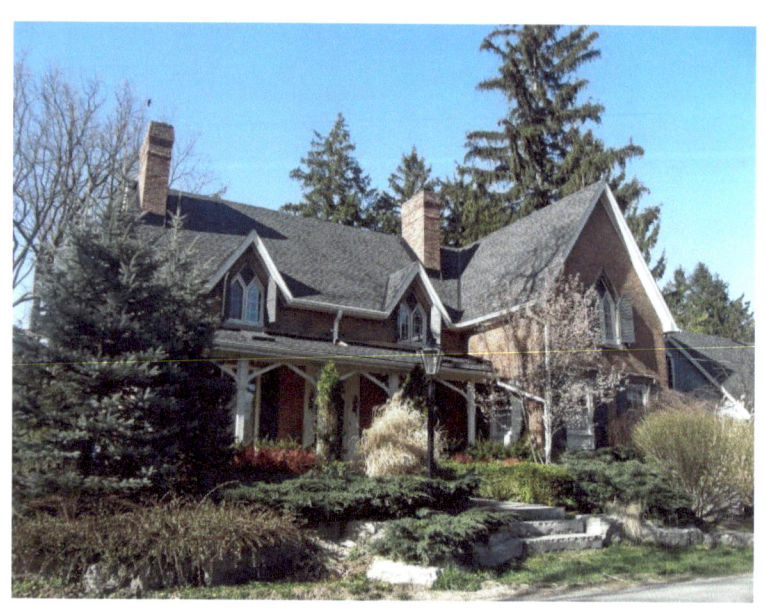

Webster's Fall Road – front view

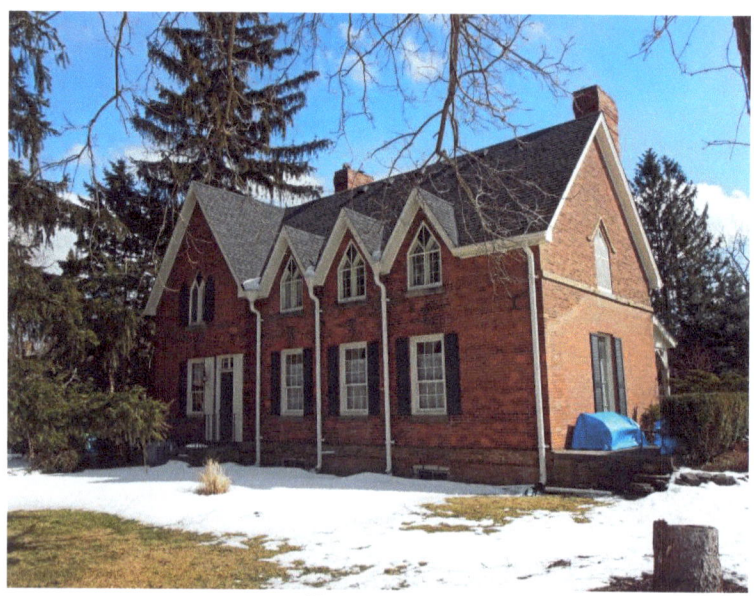

Rear view

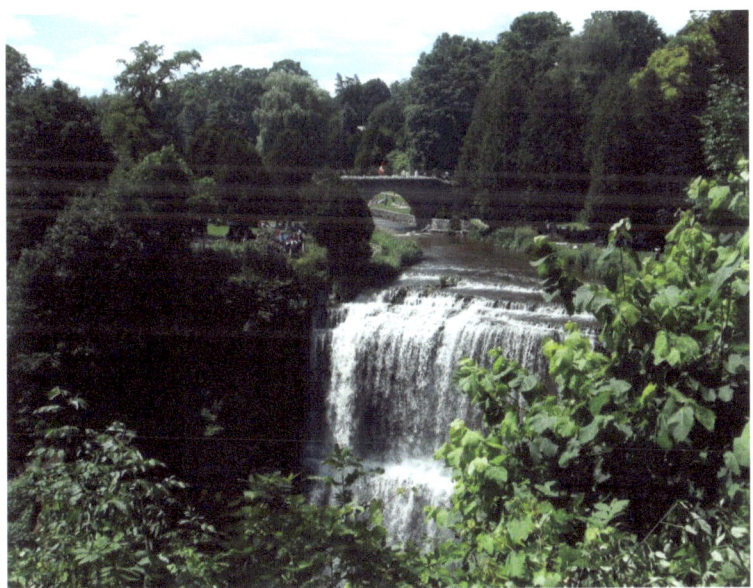

Webster's Falls with cobblestone bridge in background
Our wedding pictures were taken in the park.

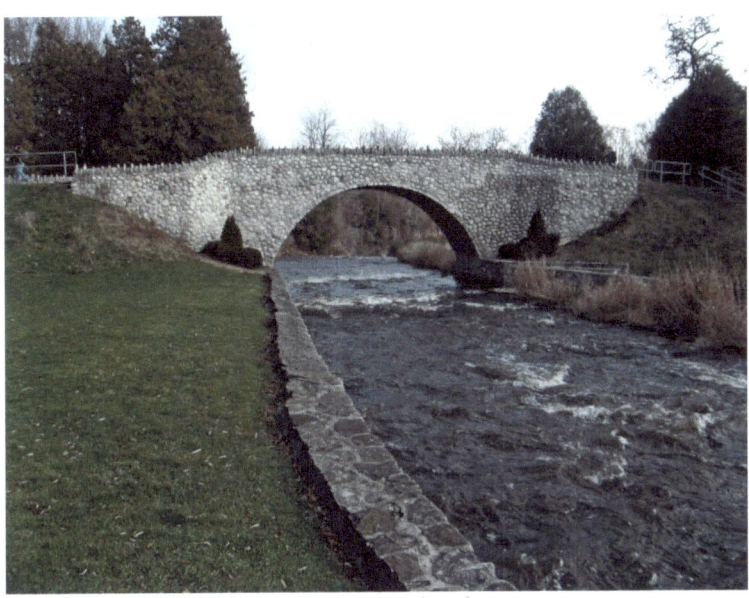

Cobblestone bridge

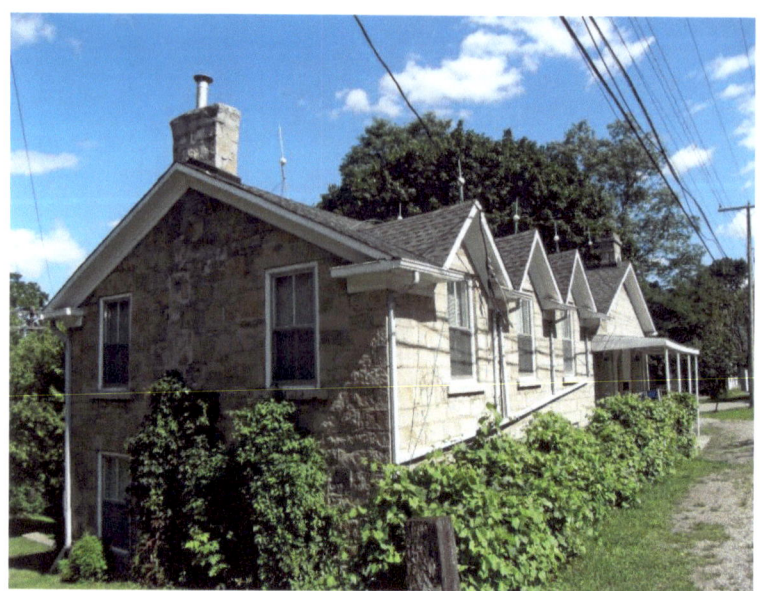

Bullock's Corners limestone house

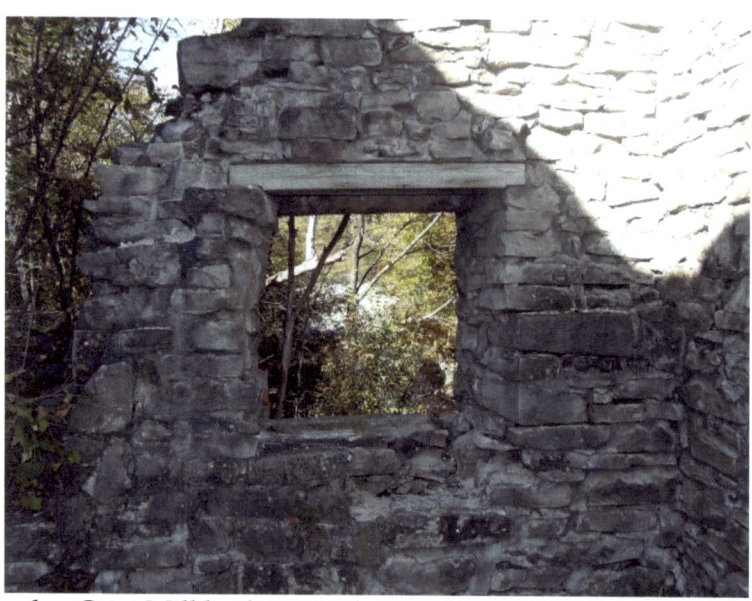

Darnley Grist Mill built 1813 of stone from quarry near Morden's Mills downstream. The building was three stories high with a 9-metre waterwheel mounted on the wall beside Spencer Creek, and had four sets of grindstones.

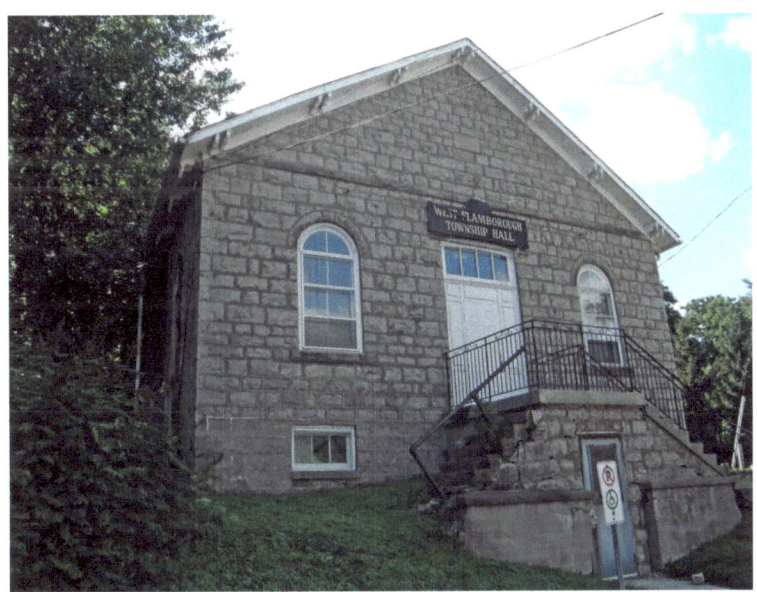

West Flamborough Township Hall
Harry and I were married here on August 13, 1972.

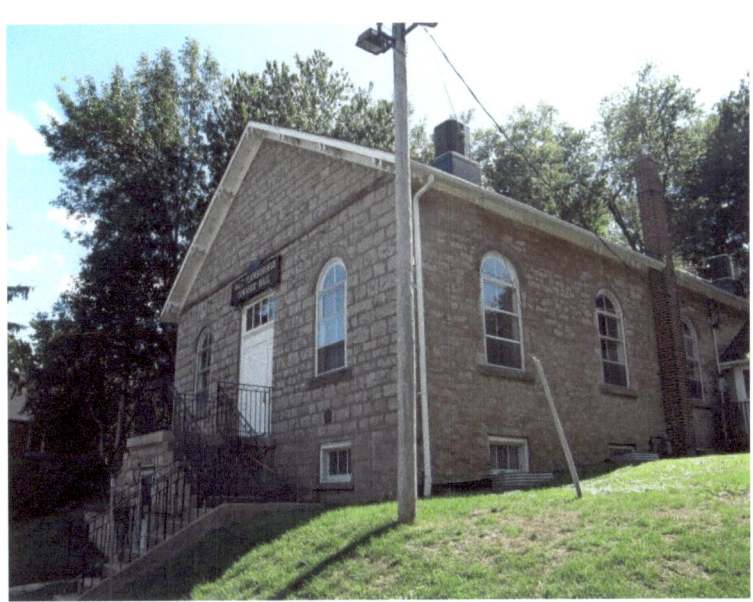

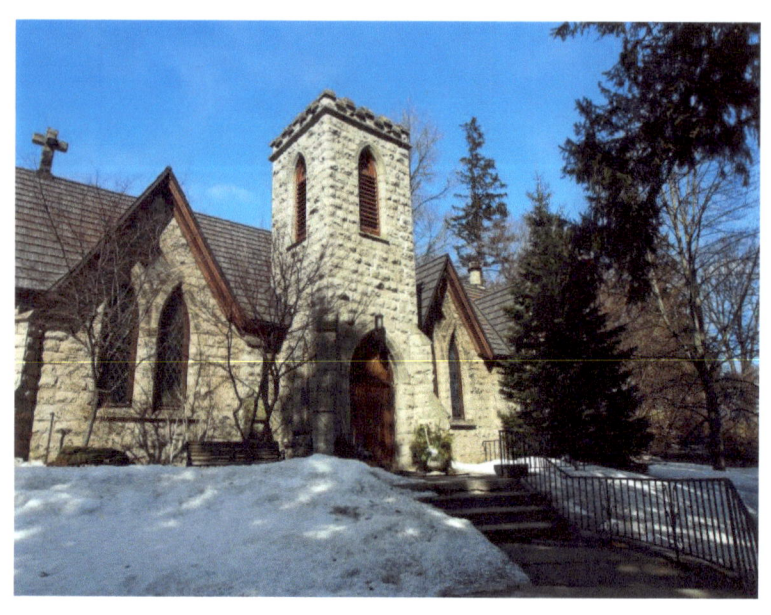

Christ Church – Anglican
90 Highway 8 at Bullock's Corners – built in 1864

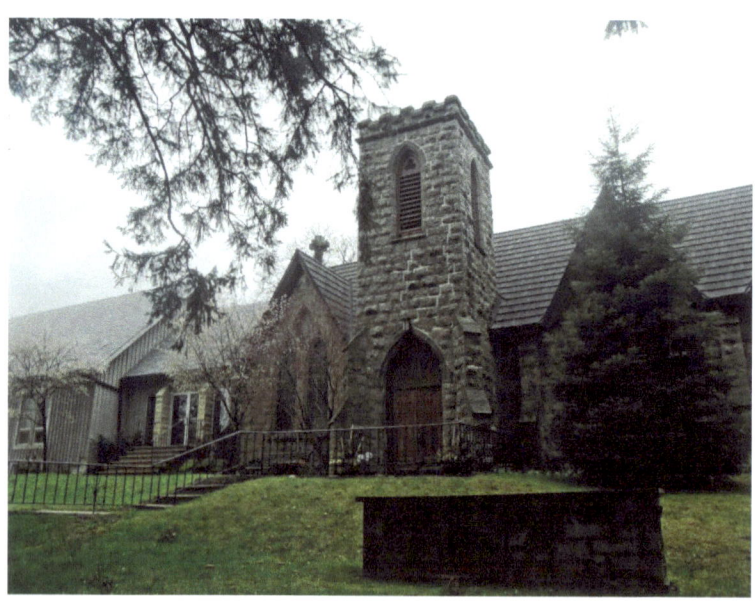

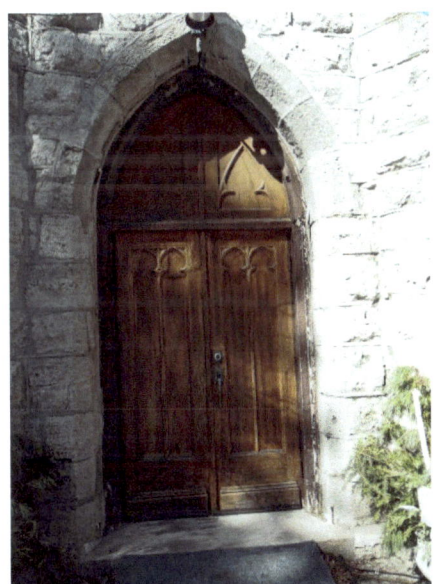

Carved door

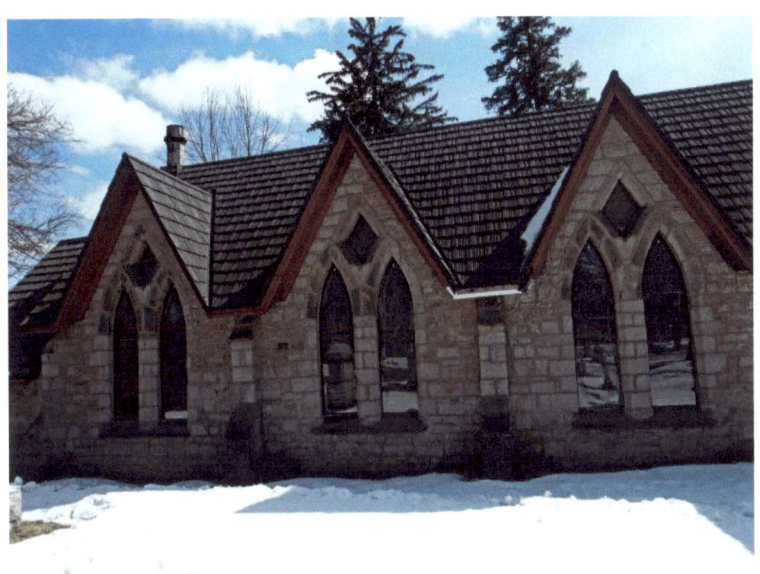

Rear view – lancet windows – Gothic arches

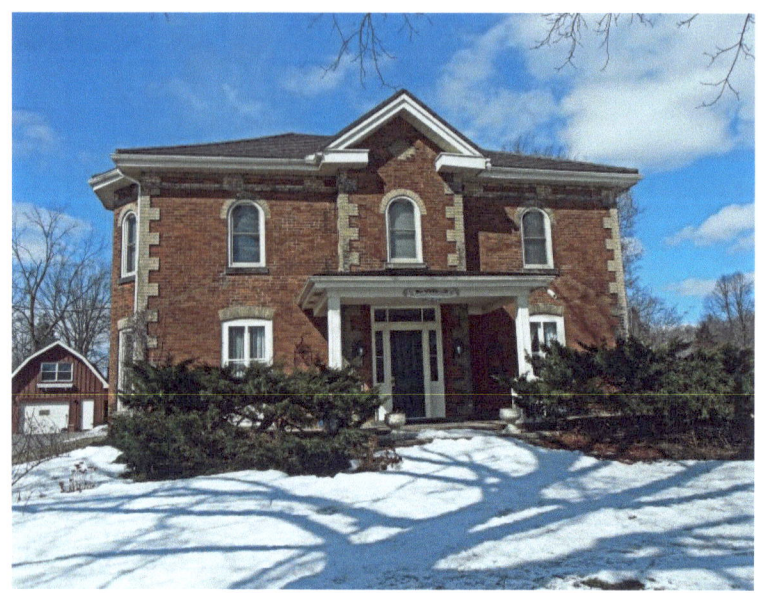

667 Harvest Road – Italianate, two-and-a-half storey frontispiece with cornice return on gable, two-storey bay window on side, corner quoins, arched window voussoirs

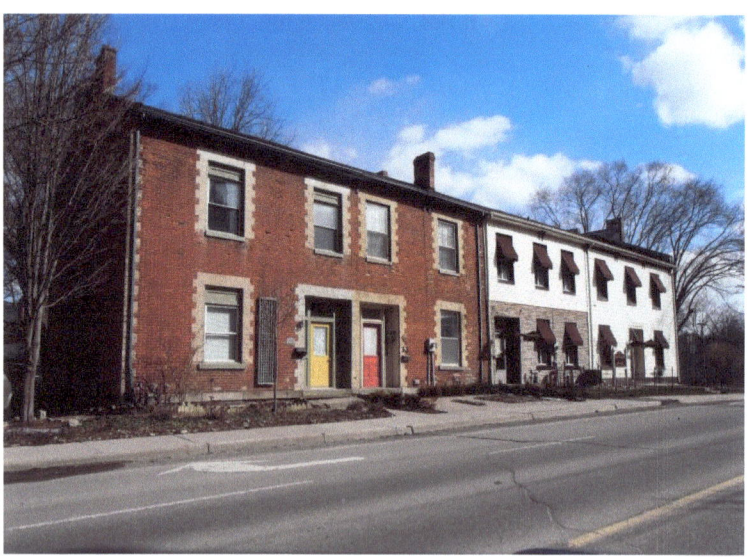

31-37 Ogilvie Street – Heritage building – c. 1860s

Cayley Street

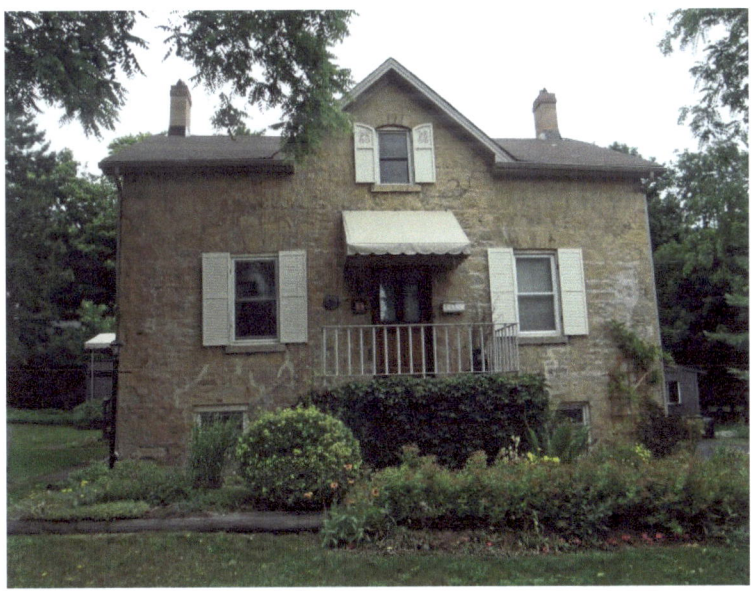

59 Cayley Street – Circa 1870s – yellow brick – Gothic Revival

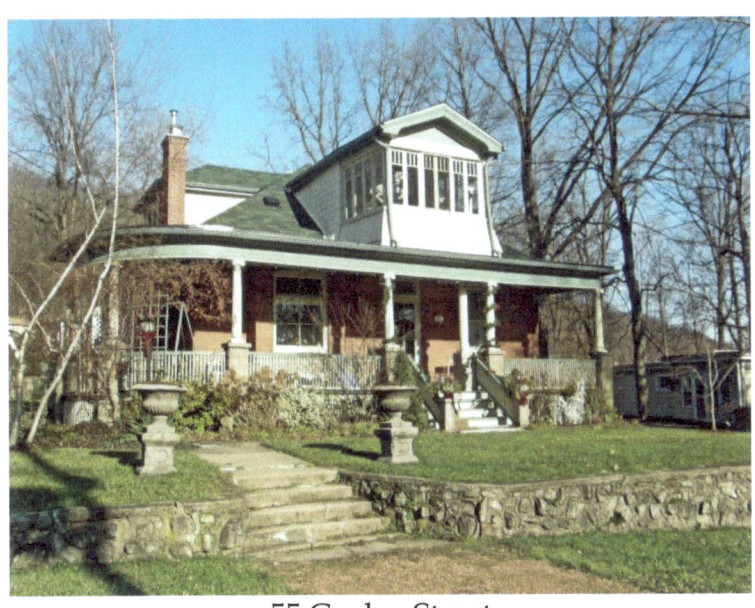

55 Cayley Street

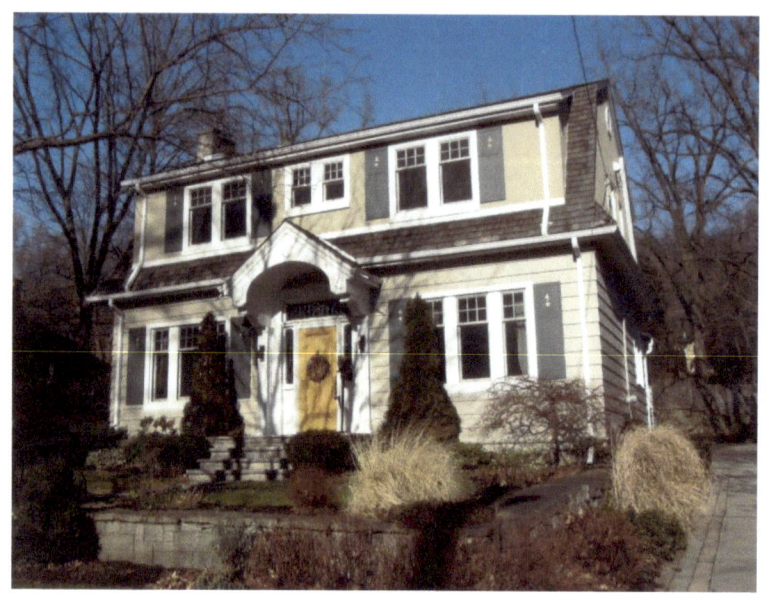

51 Cayley Street

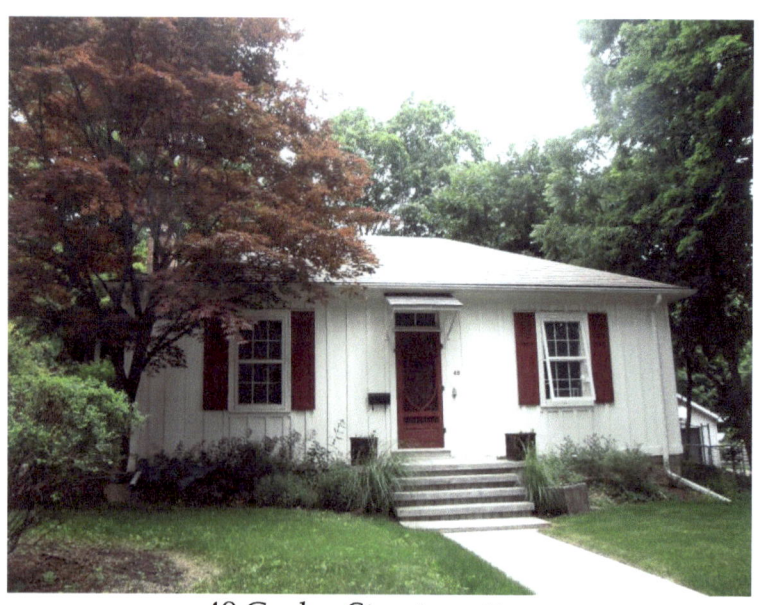

49 Cayley Street - cottage

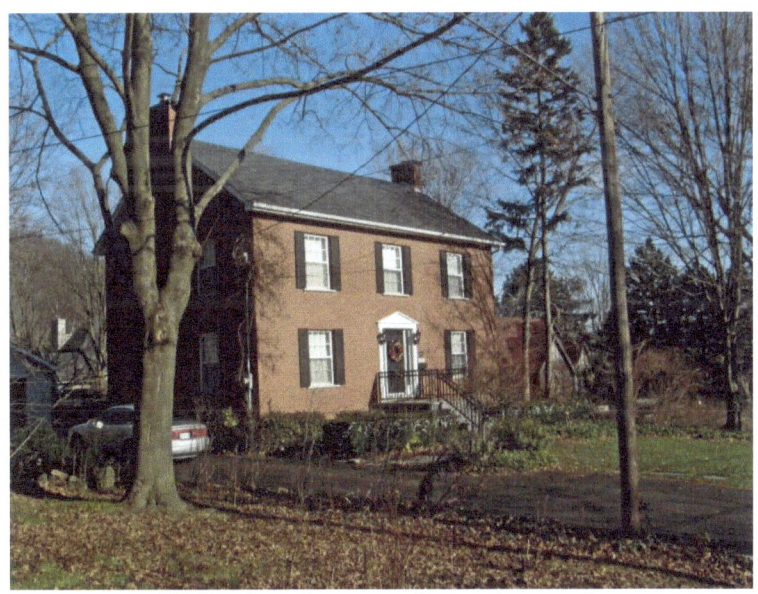

37 Cayley Street – Georgian style

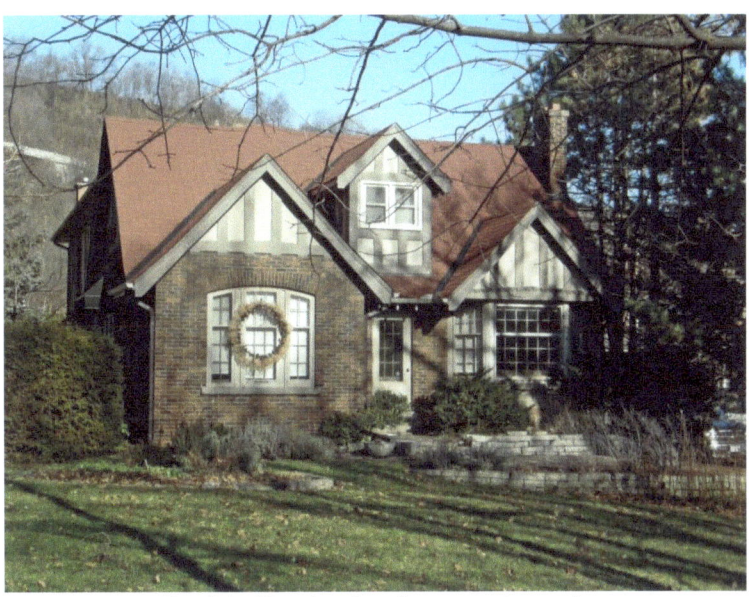

Gothic Revival – dormer in attic

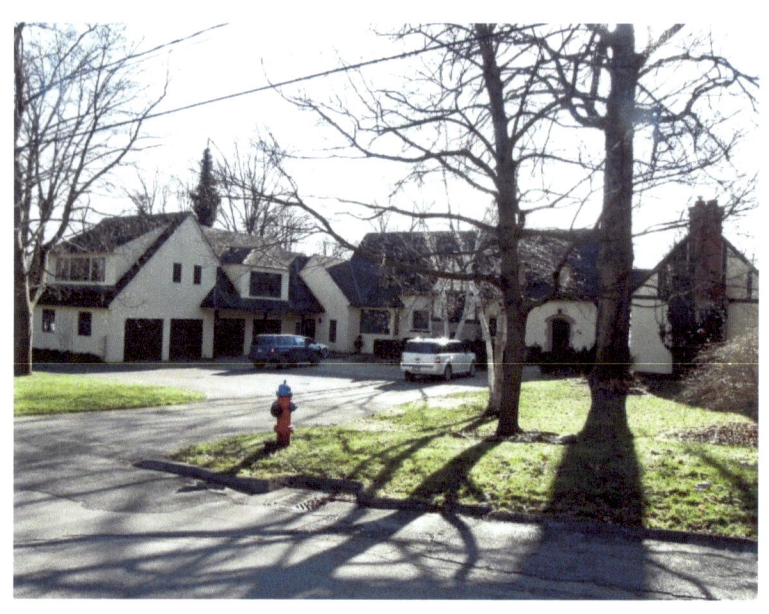

36 Cayley Street

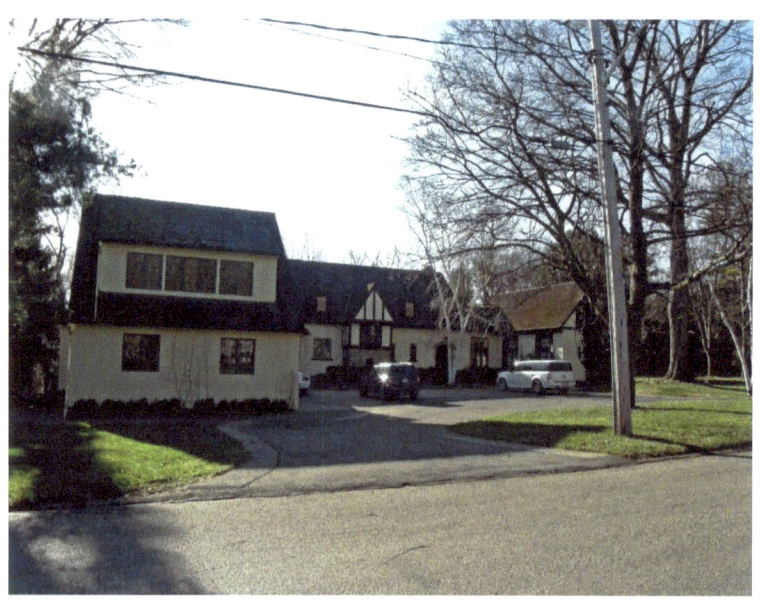

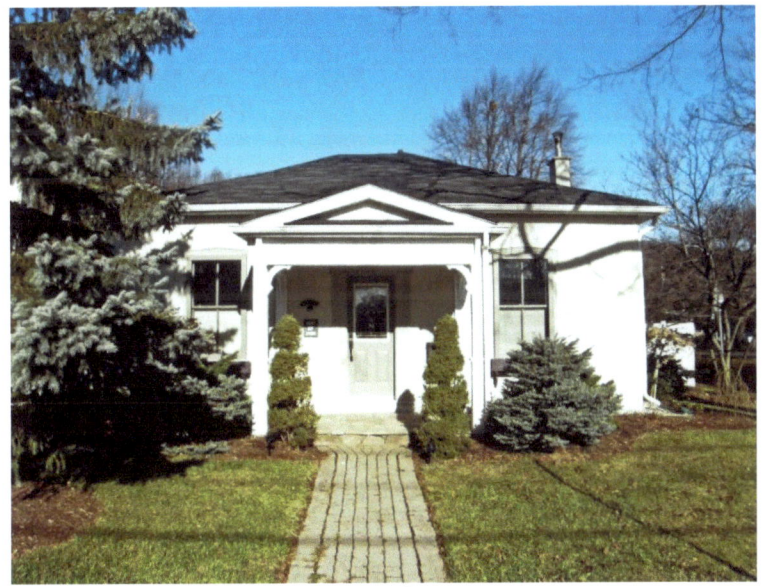

Regency Cottage

Parkview Street

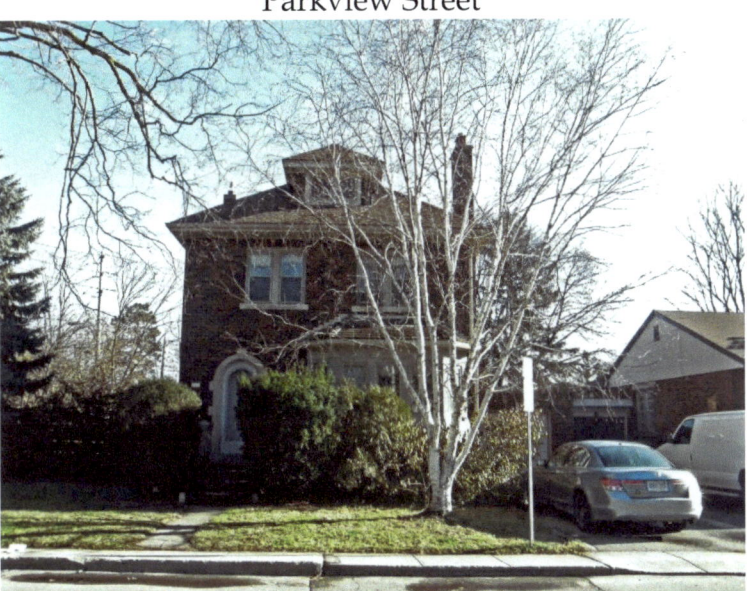

Italianate, dormer in attic

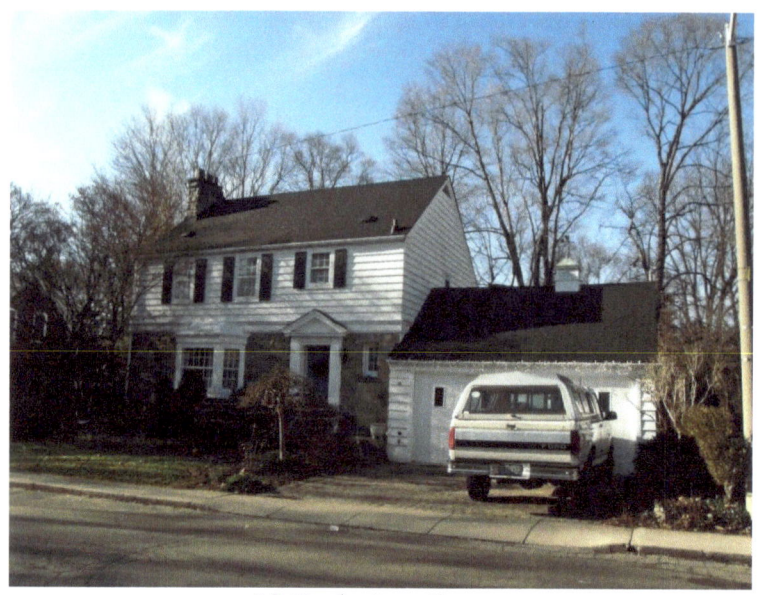

12 Parkview Street

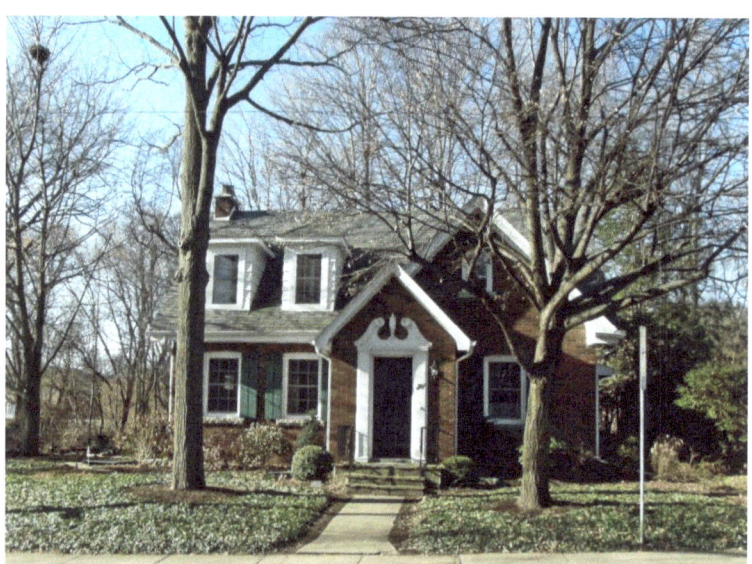

10 Parkview Street – Gothic Revival, dormers in attic

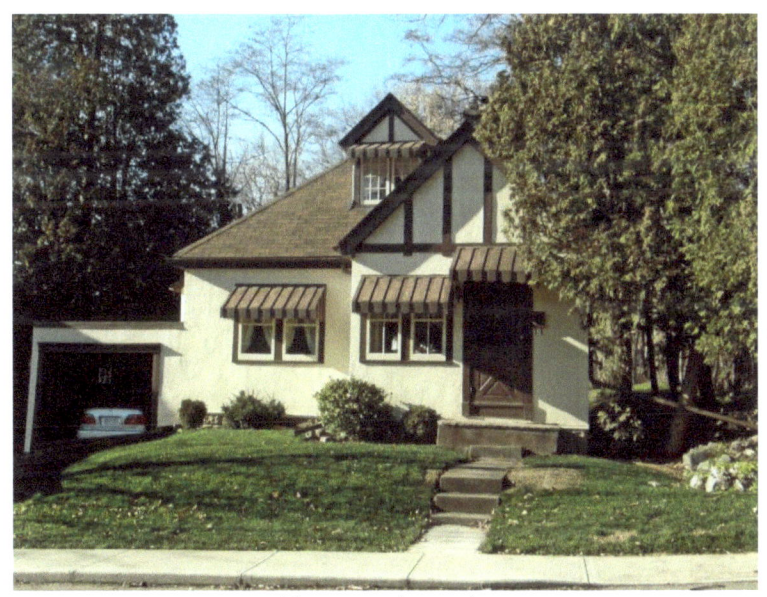

Dormer in attic

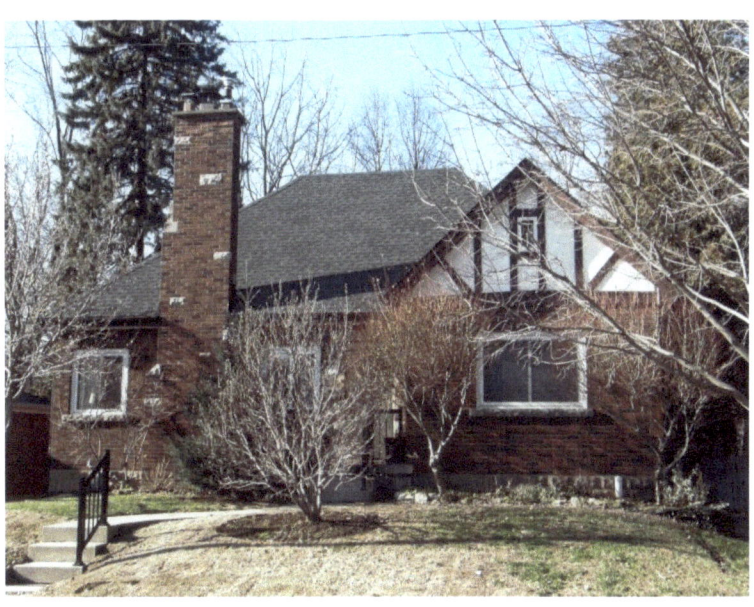

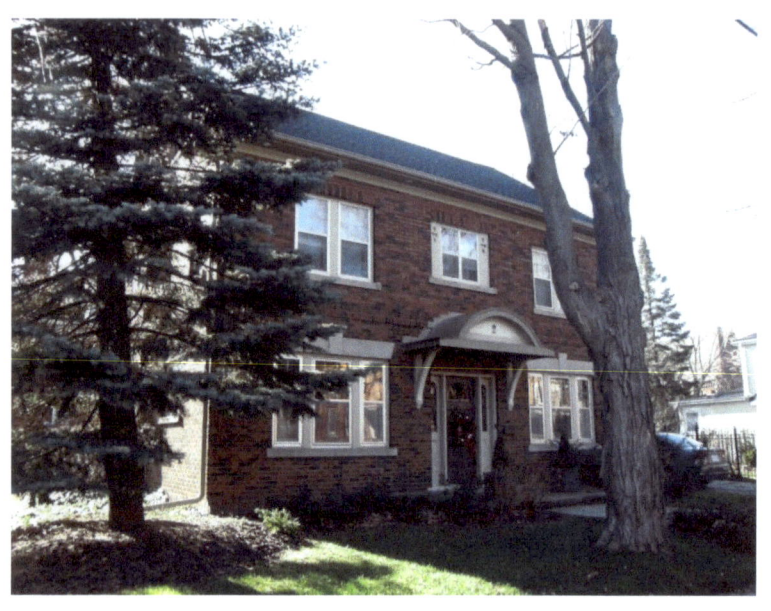

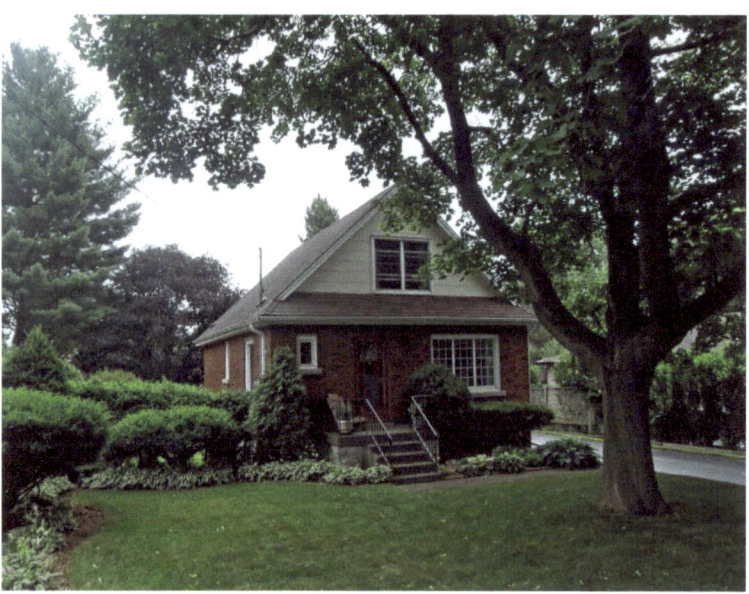

Hillside – one-and-a-half storey

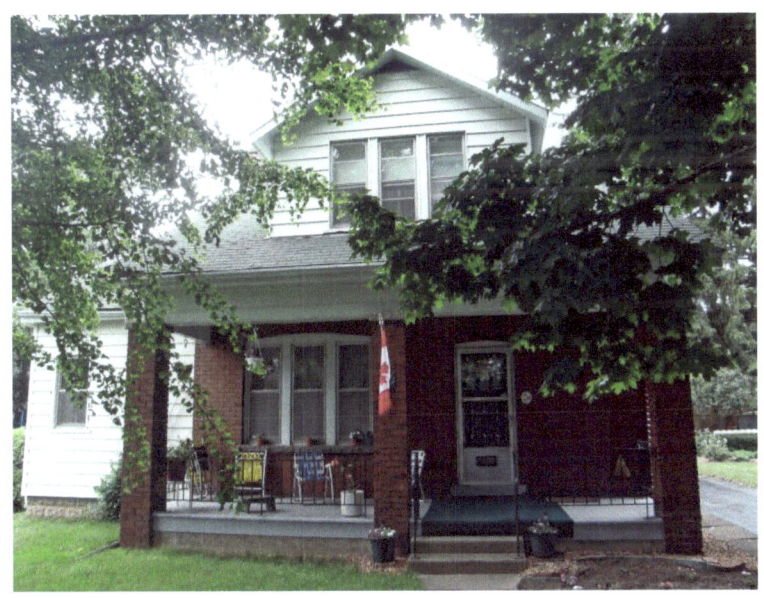

30 Hillside – built early 1930s

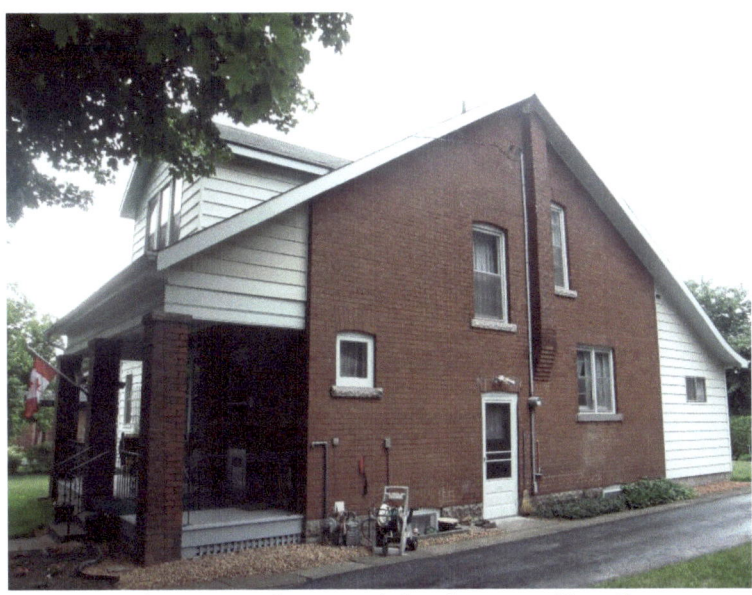

side view – home of the Stewart Family

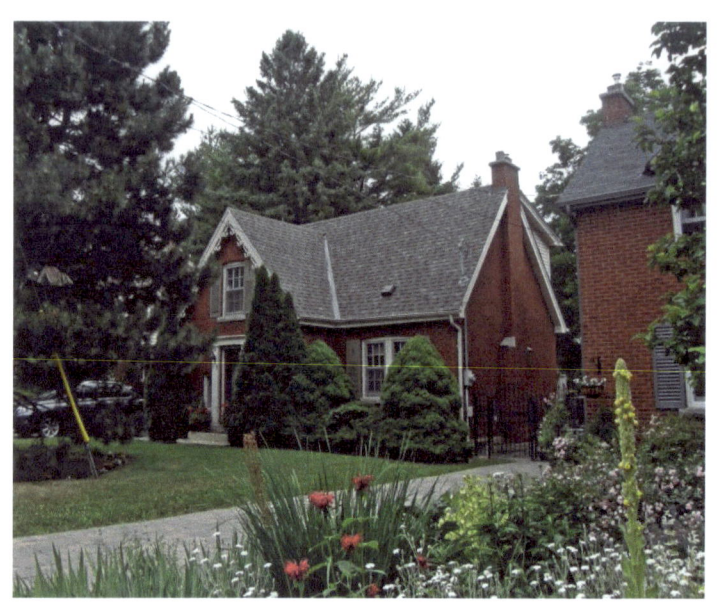

13 Hillside
Gingerbread trim on the gable

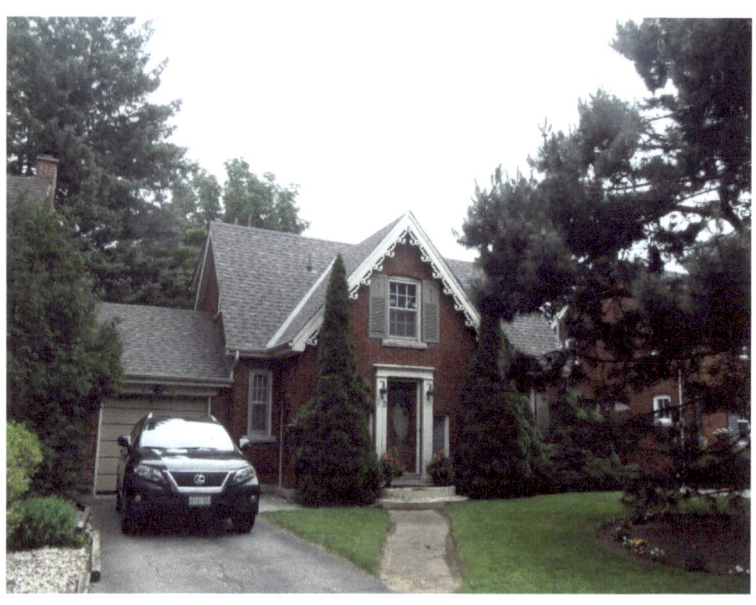

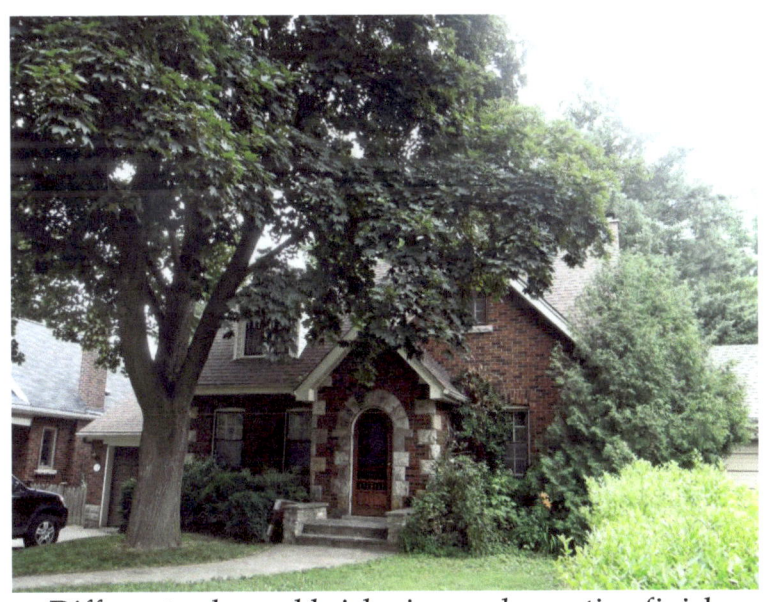

Different coloured brick gives a decorative finish
around the entrance

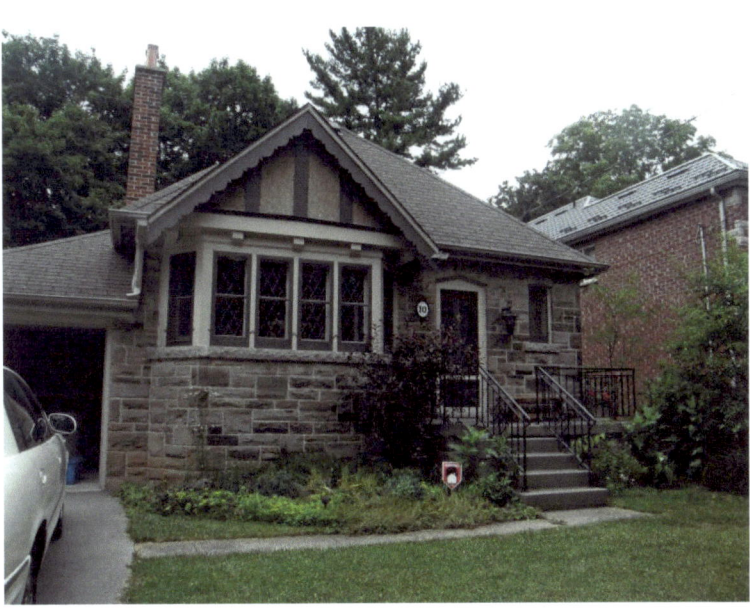

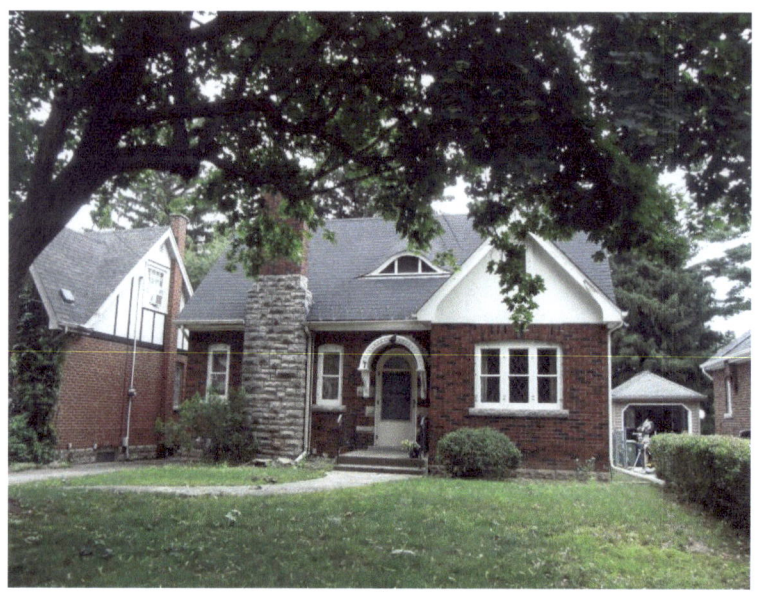

7 Hillside

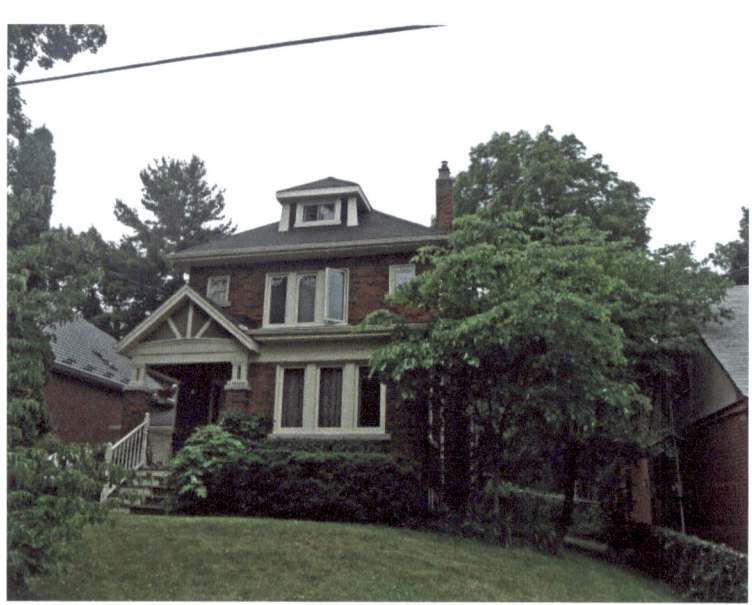

6 Hillside – Italianate – dormer in attic

South Street Area

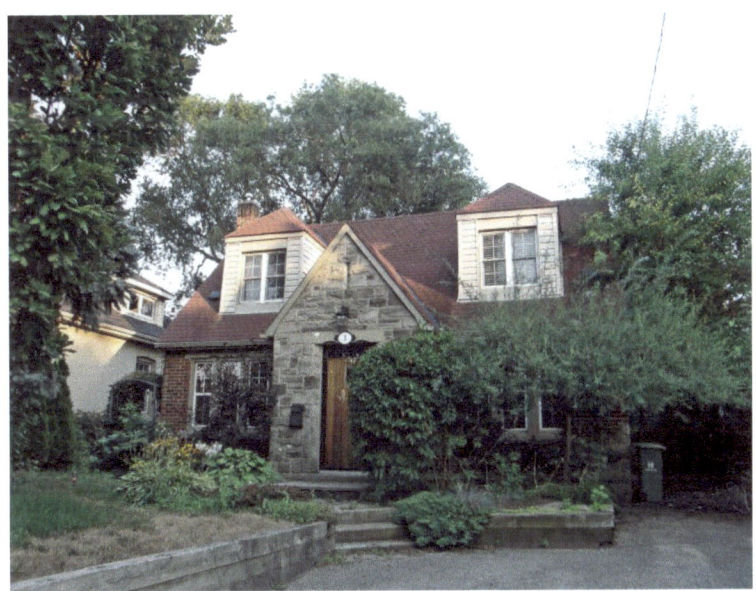

3 South Street – dormers in attic

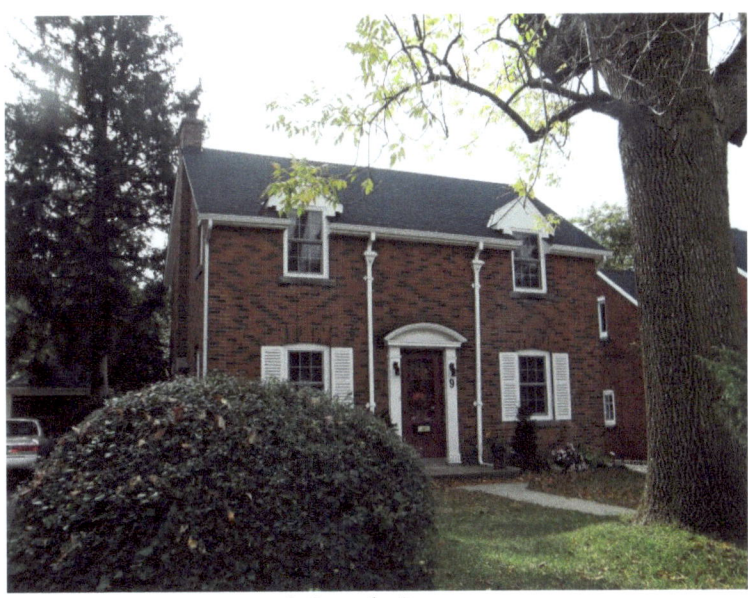

9 South Street

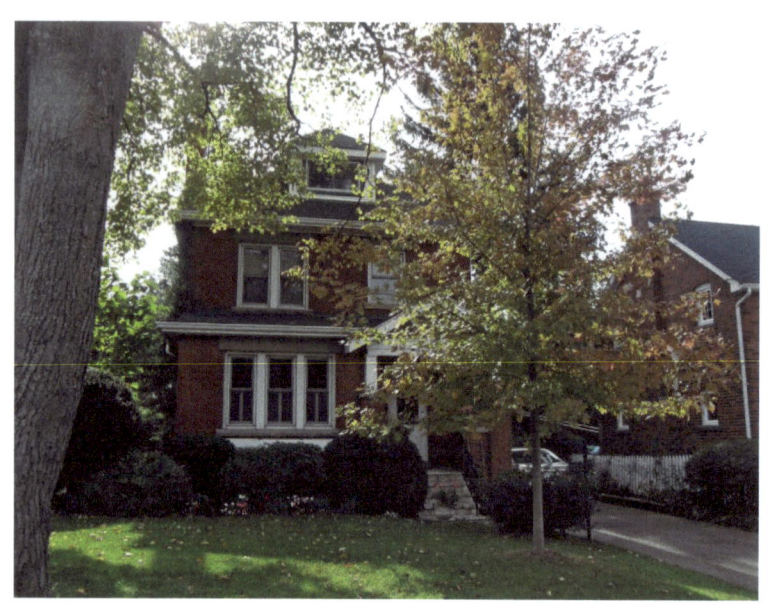

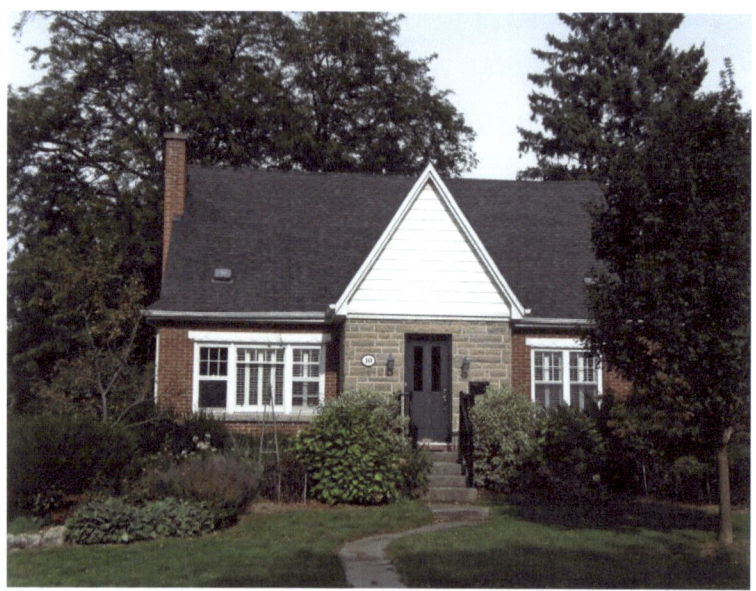

10 South Street

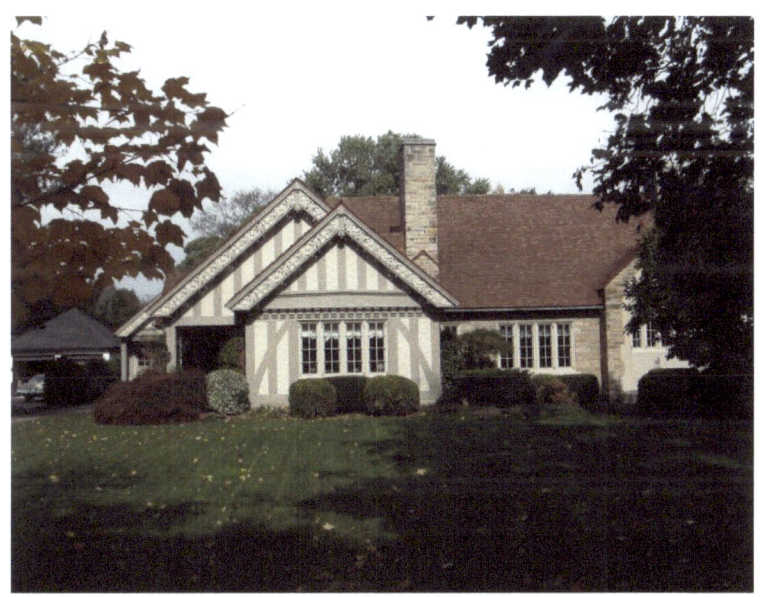

67 South Street – Tudor style trim

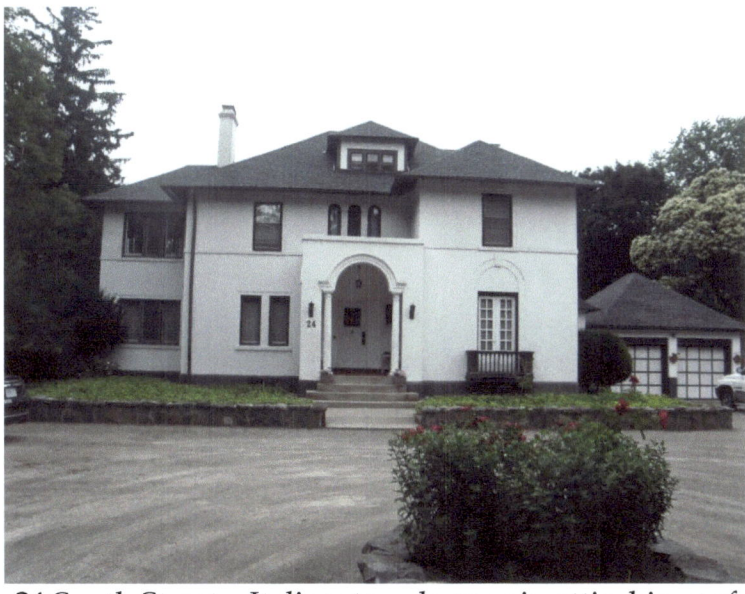

24 South Street – Italianate – dormer in attic, hip roof

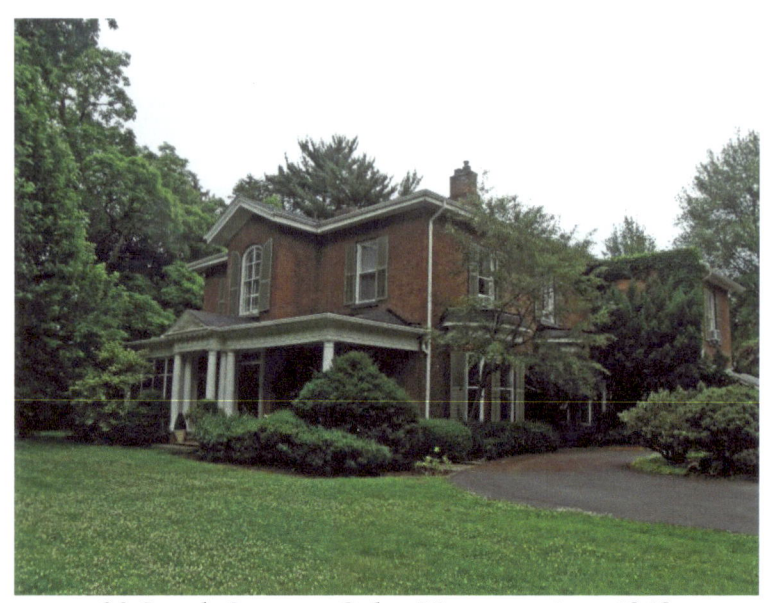

30 South Street – Osler House – circa 1848
Italianate with two-storey tower-like bay

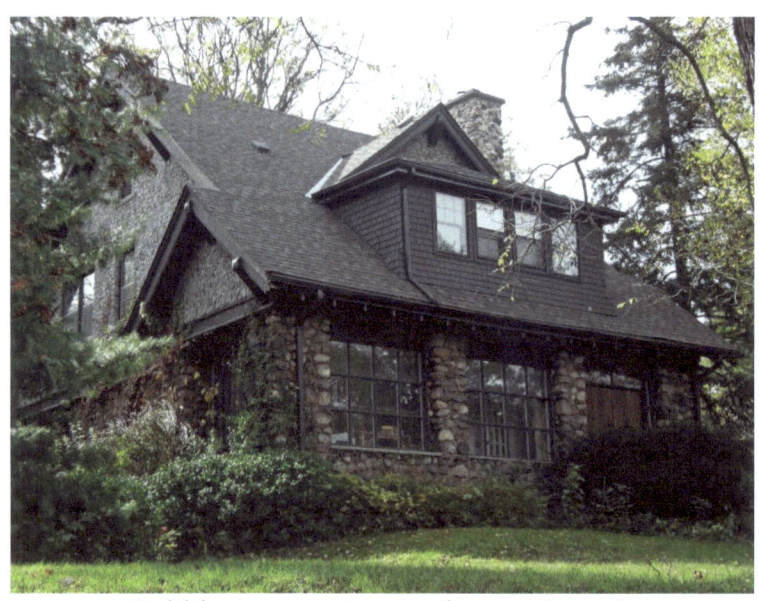

Cobblestone cottage – dormer in attic

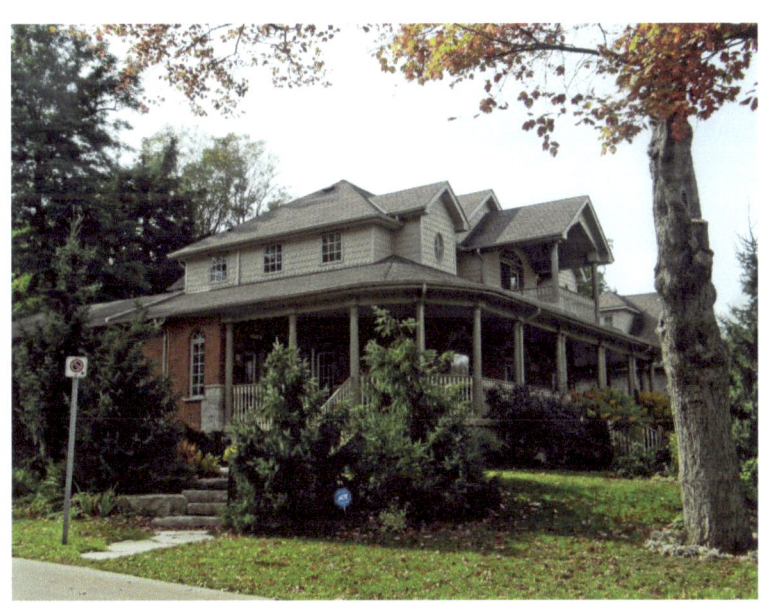

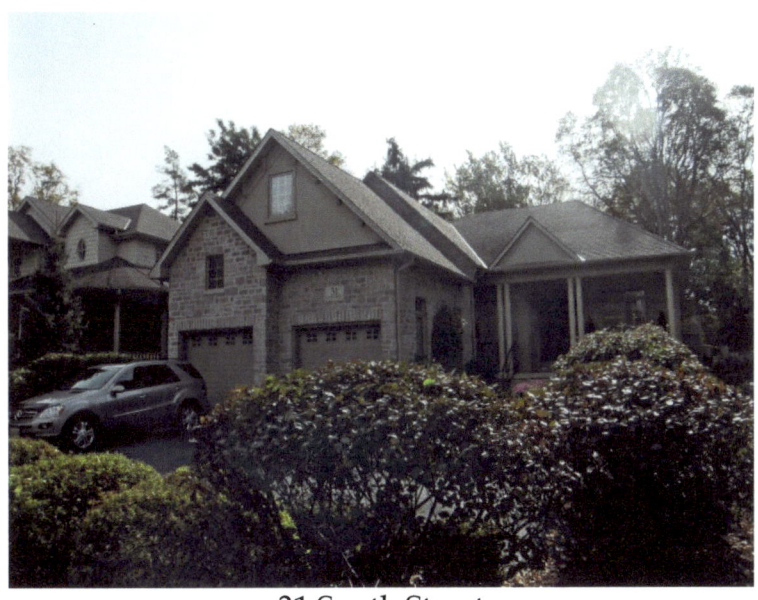

31 South Street

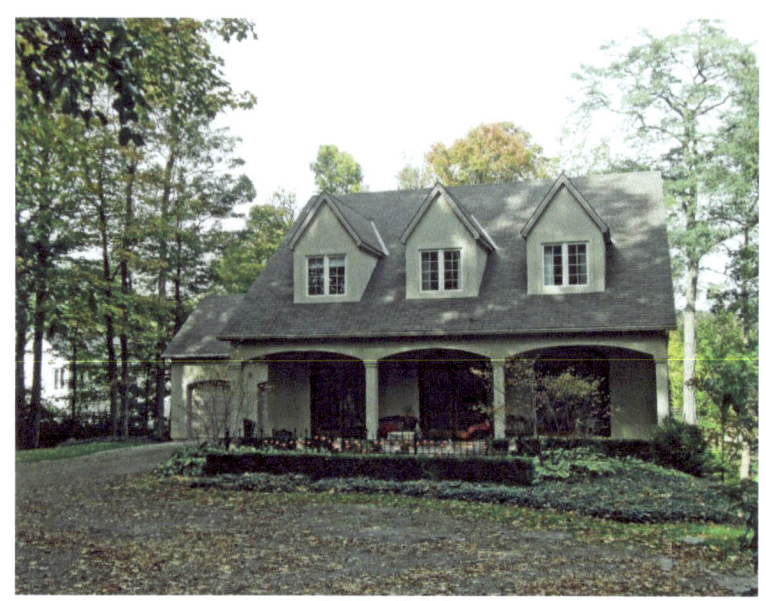

9 Hatfield

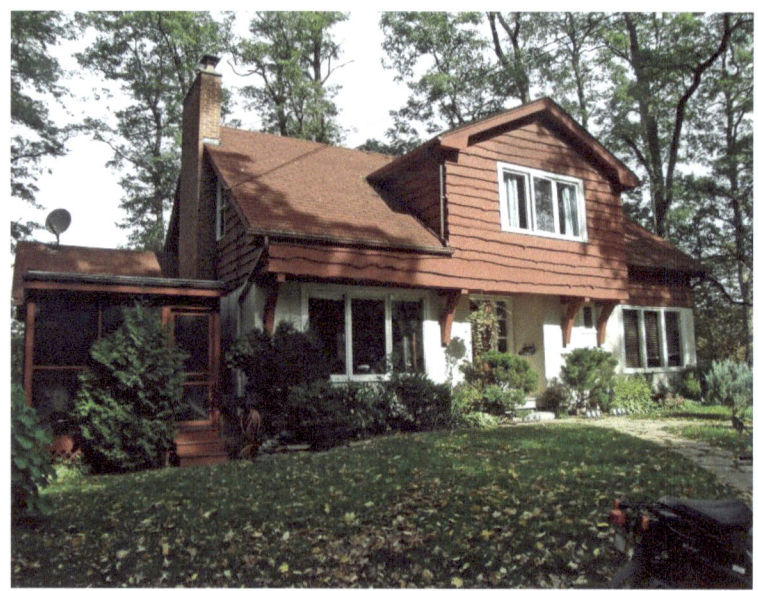

7 Hatfield

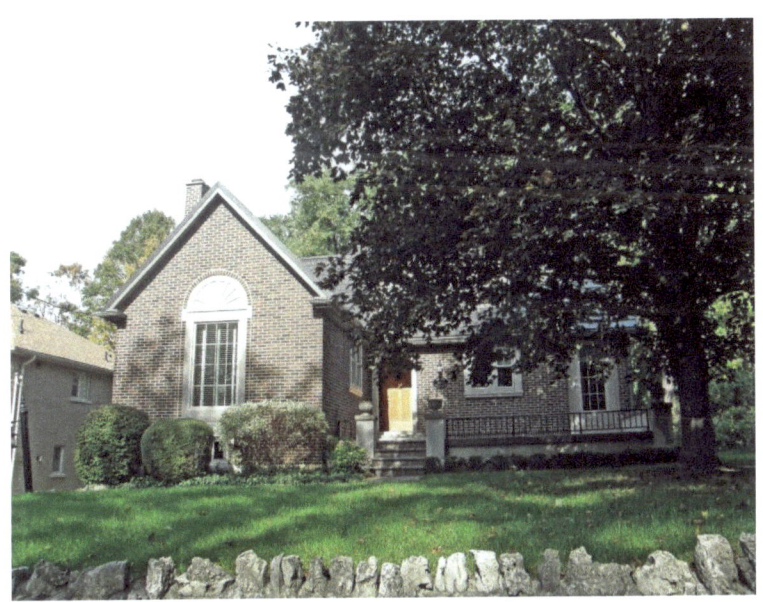

64 South Street - Devon Cottage

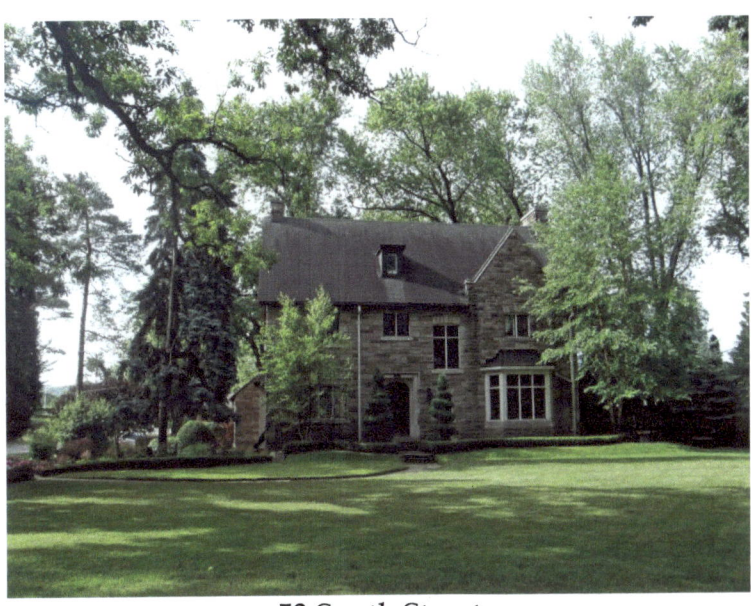

53 South Street

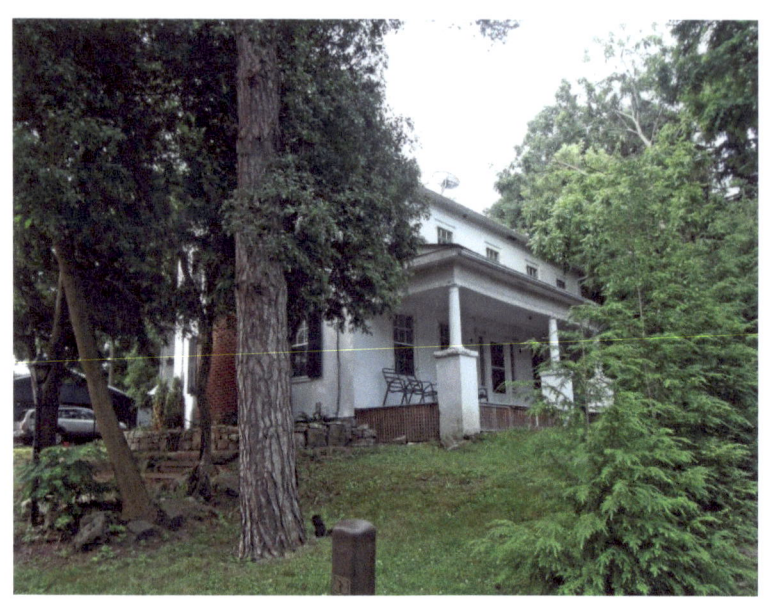

6 Woodward

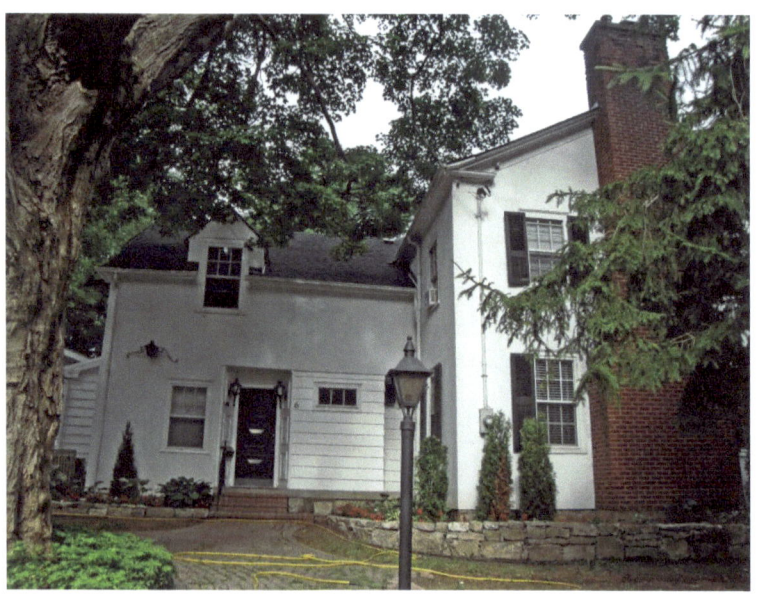

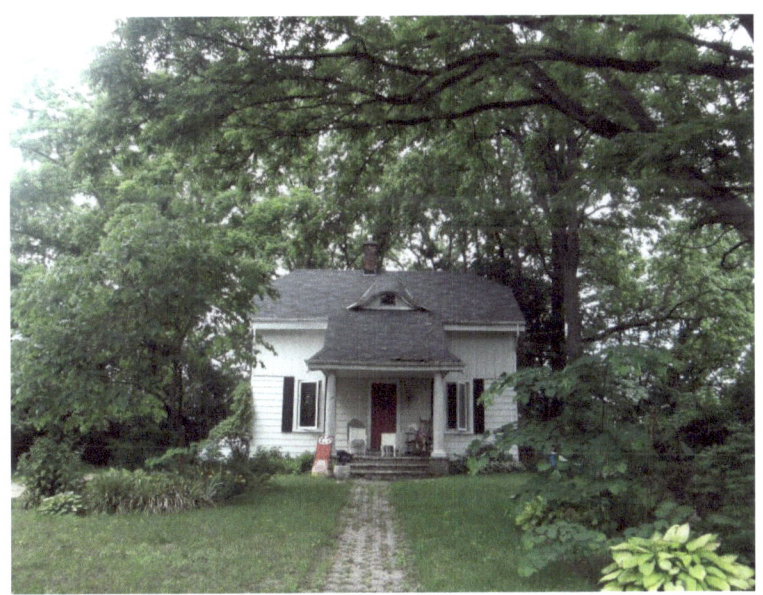

10 Woodward

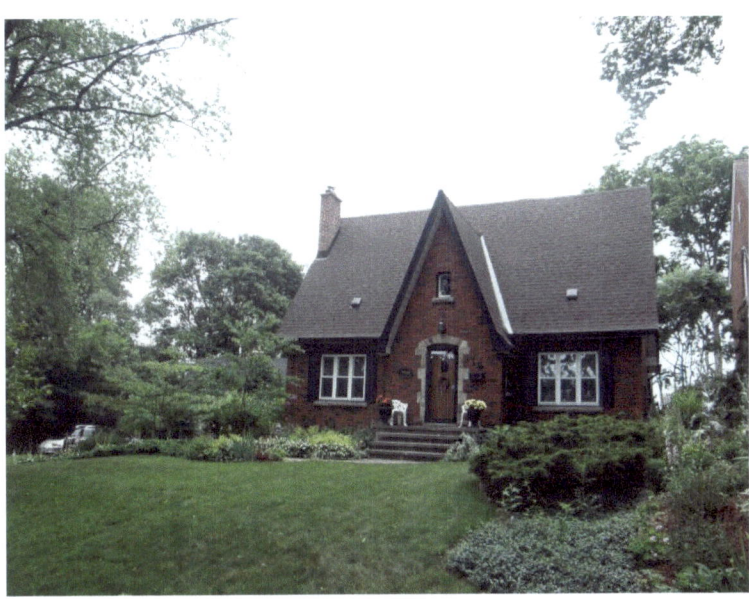

Valleyhill – 16 Woodward

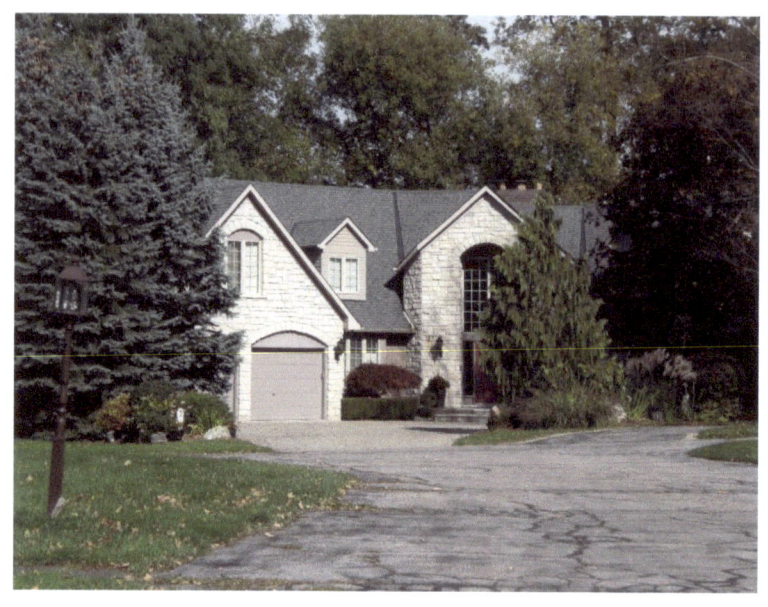

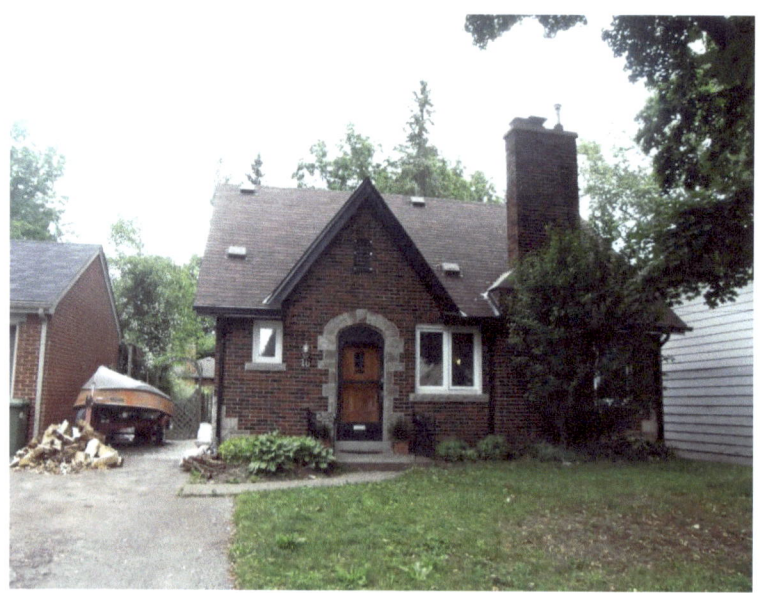

#16

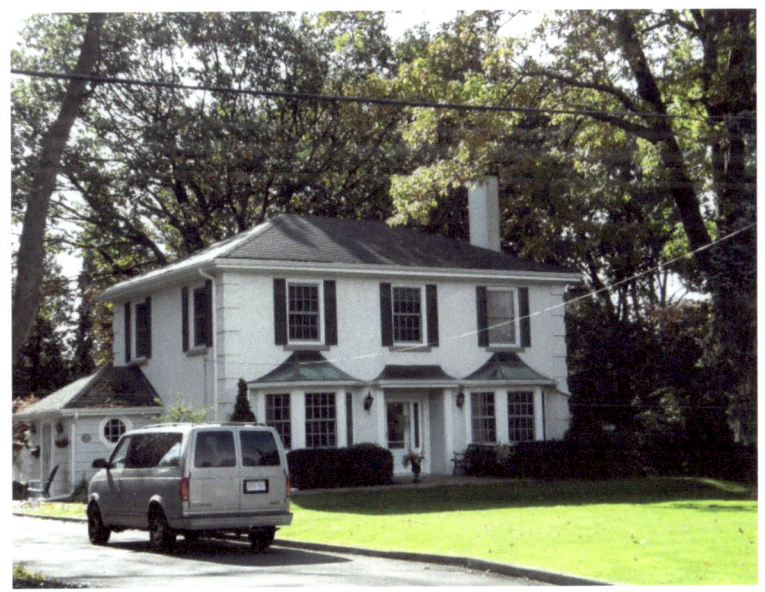

75 South Street – Italianate, hip roof

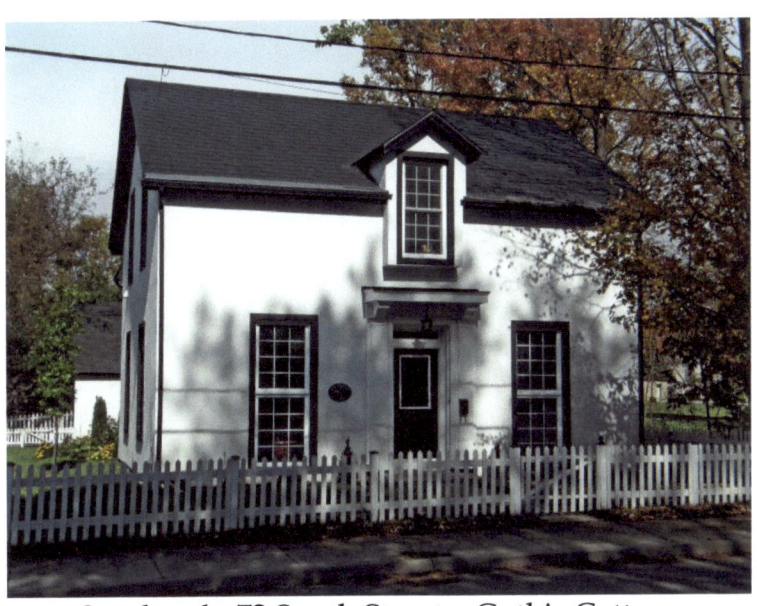

Southend - 72 South Street – Gothic Cottage

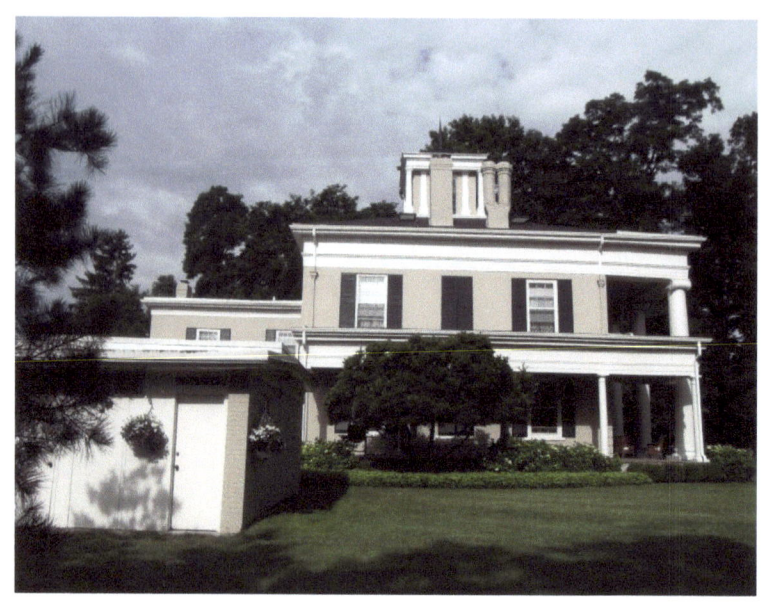

South Street

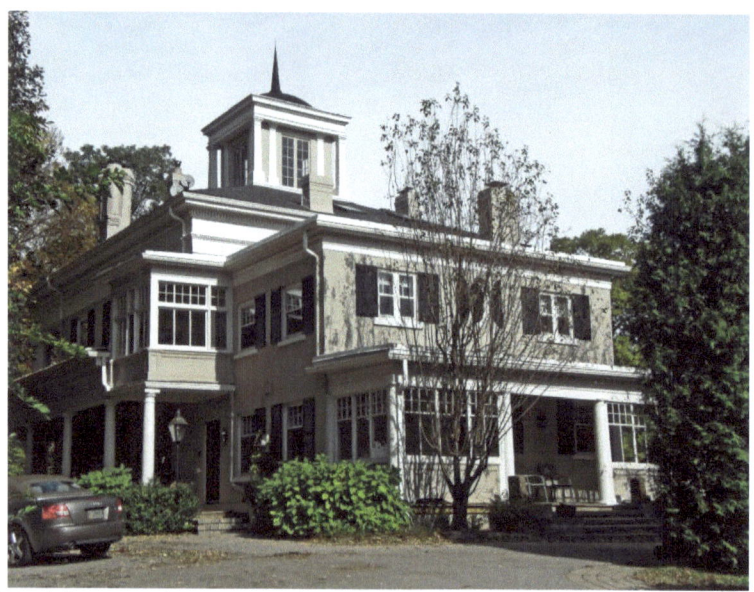

"Wedding Cake House" – Italianate – belvedere on rooftop

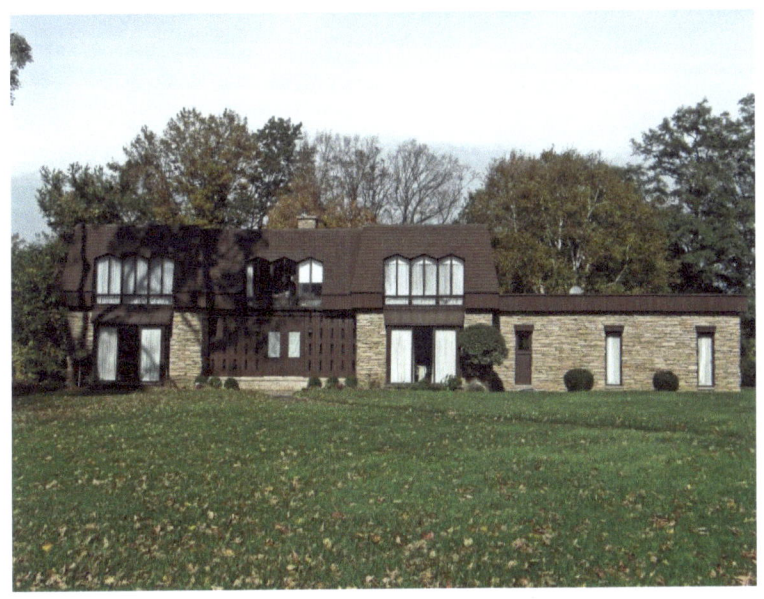

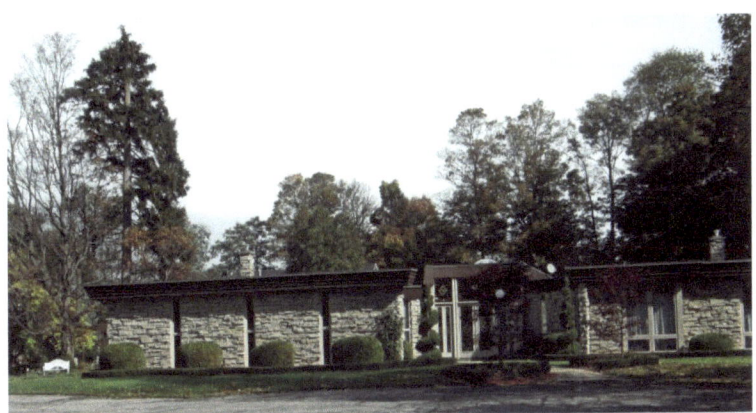

66 South Street

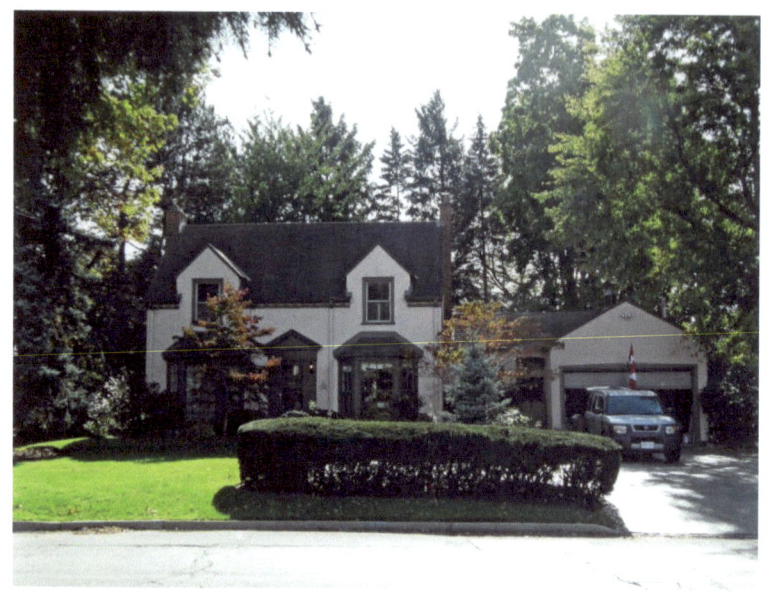

Two gables

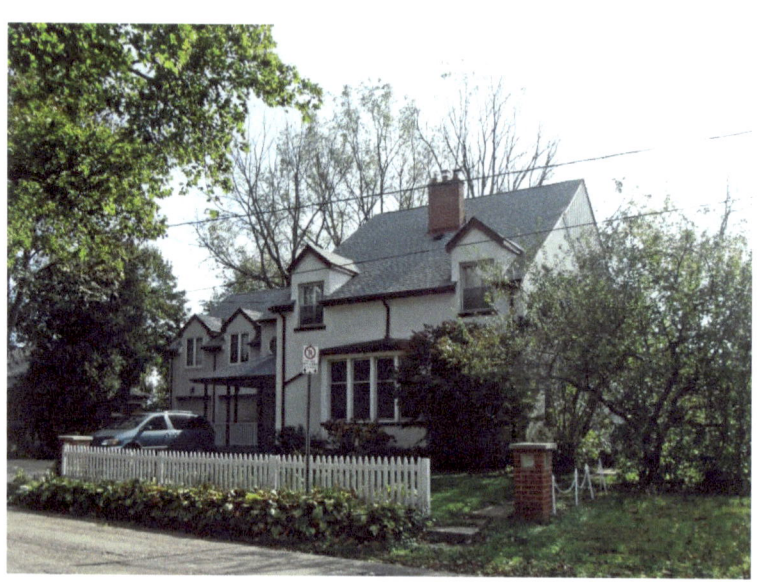

Old Ancaster Road was the main road between
Dundas and Ancaster in the early 1800s

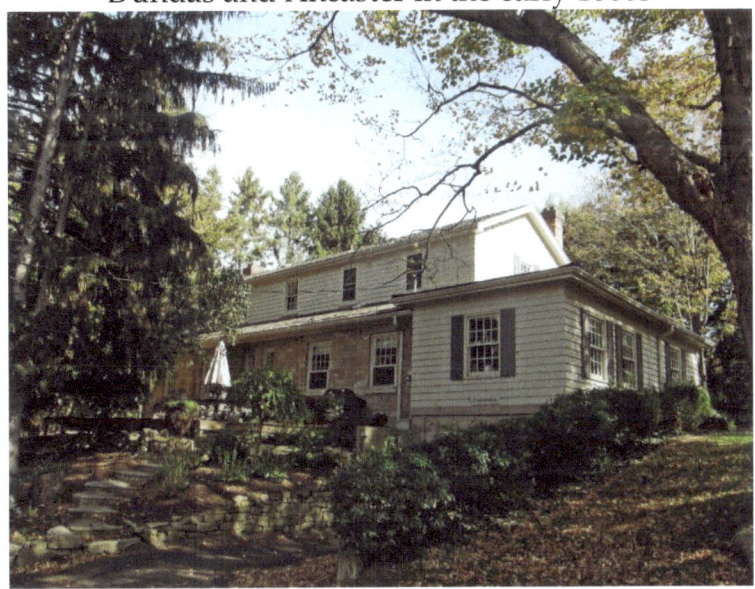

Back – 2nd storey added in 1950
12 Old Ancaster Road

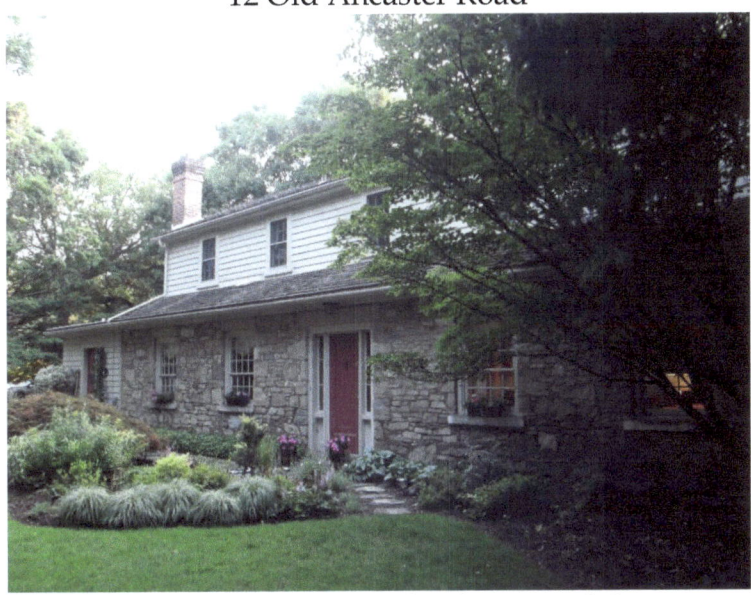

Front – built in 1940 by Mr. Holt who owned the grist mill
and brewery down the hill in Dundas

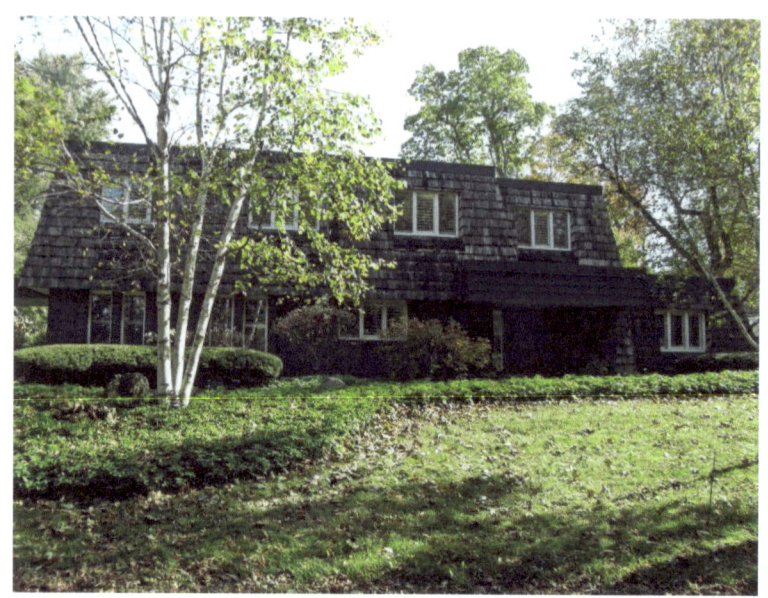

14 Old Ancaster Road

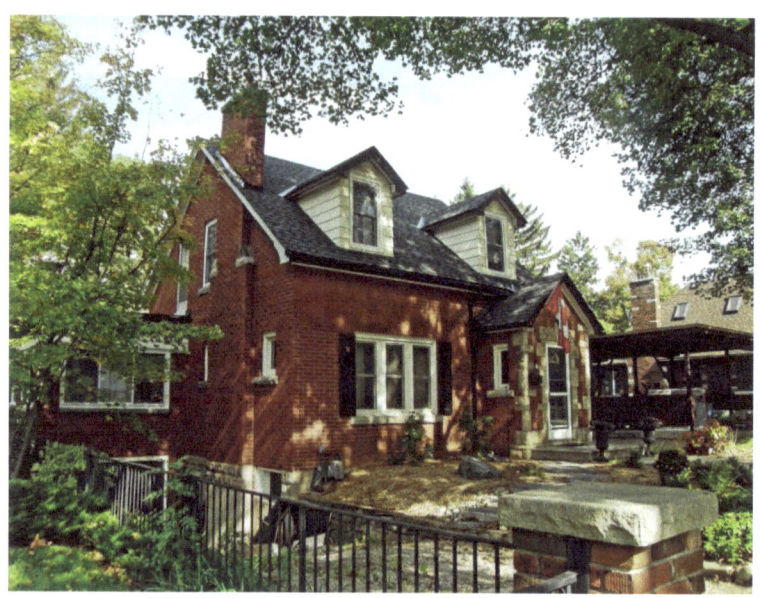

#4

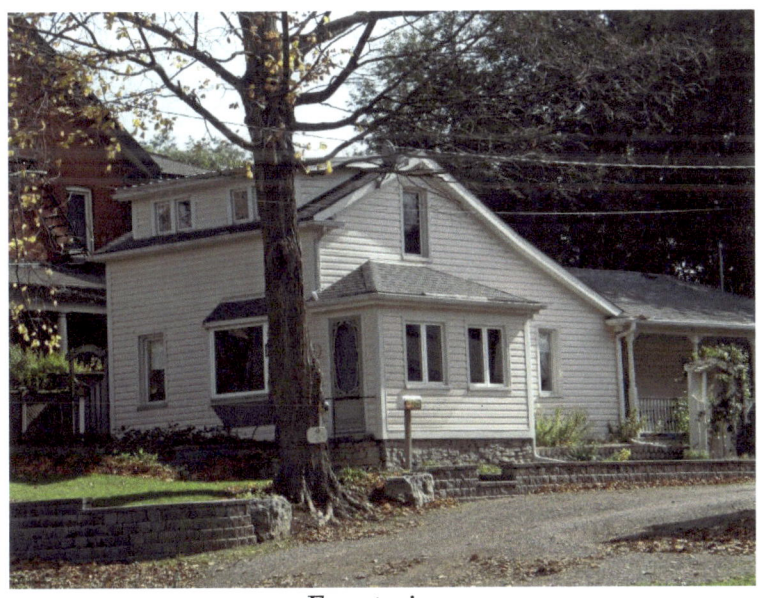

Front view

#45 – two views

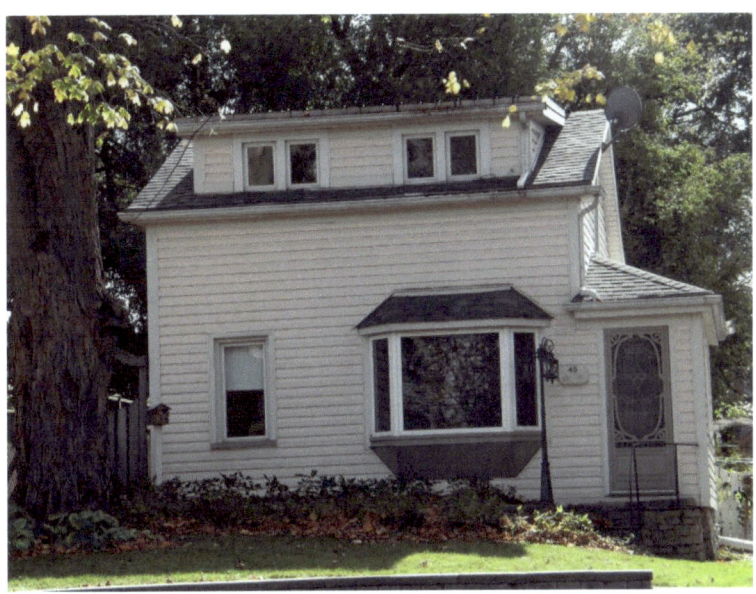

End view

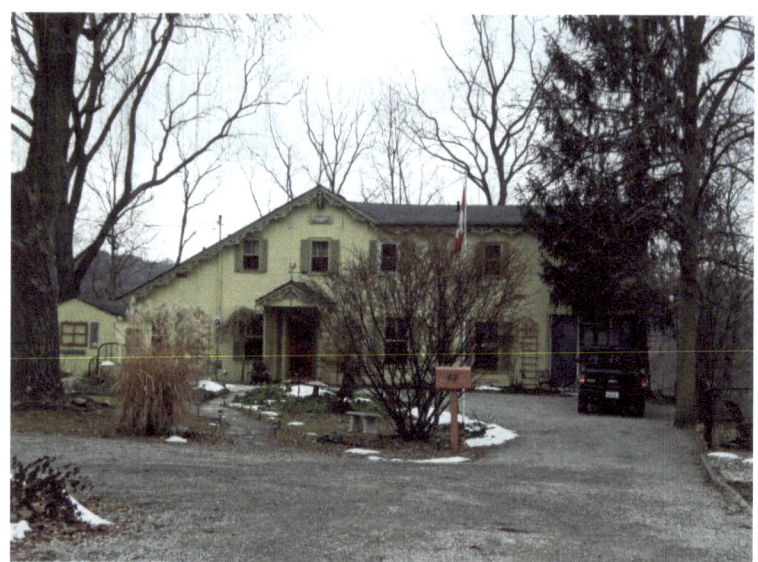

42 Osler Drive – a Bed and Breakfast called Glenwood

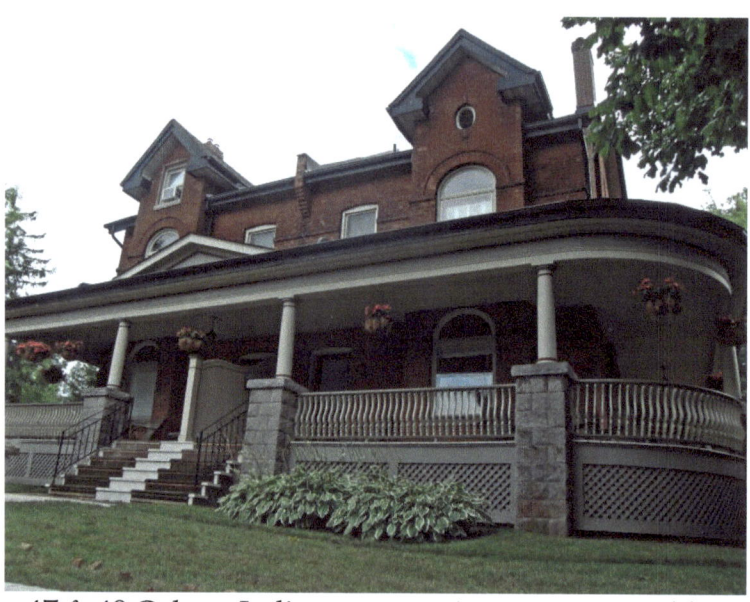

47 & 49 Osler – Italianate - cornice return on gables

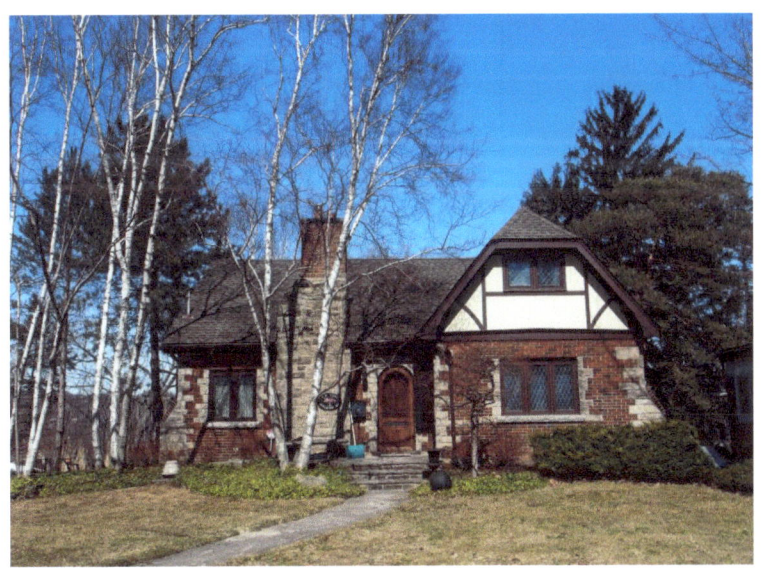

2 Ancaster Street

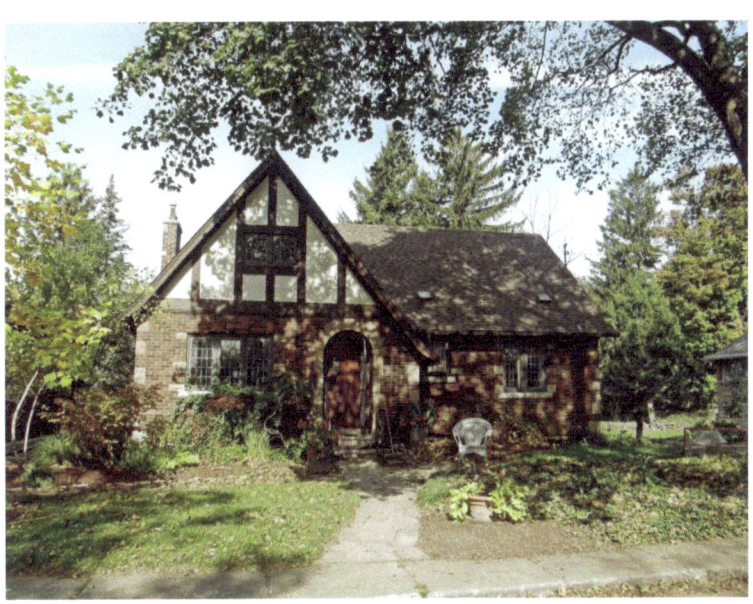

6 Ancaster Street – Tudor style

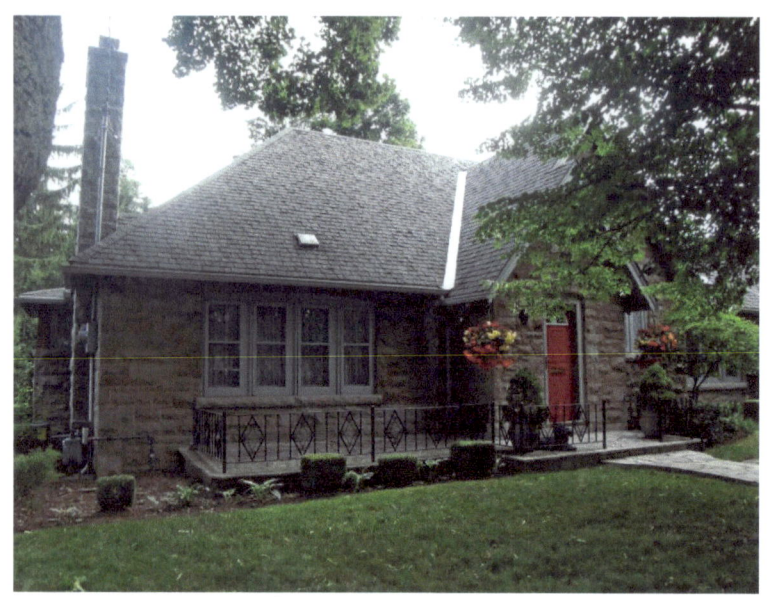

8 Ancaster Street

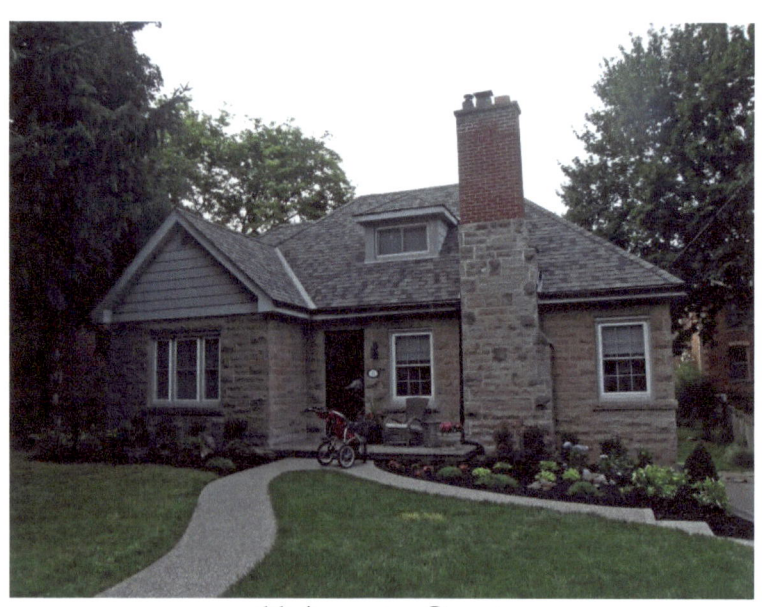

11 Ancaster Street

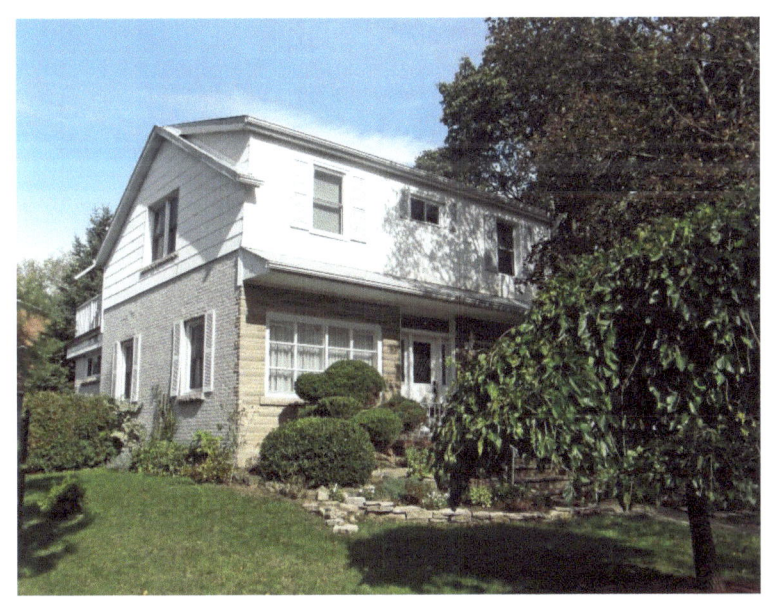

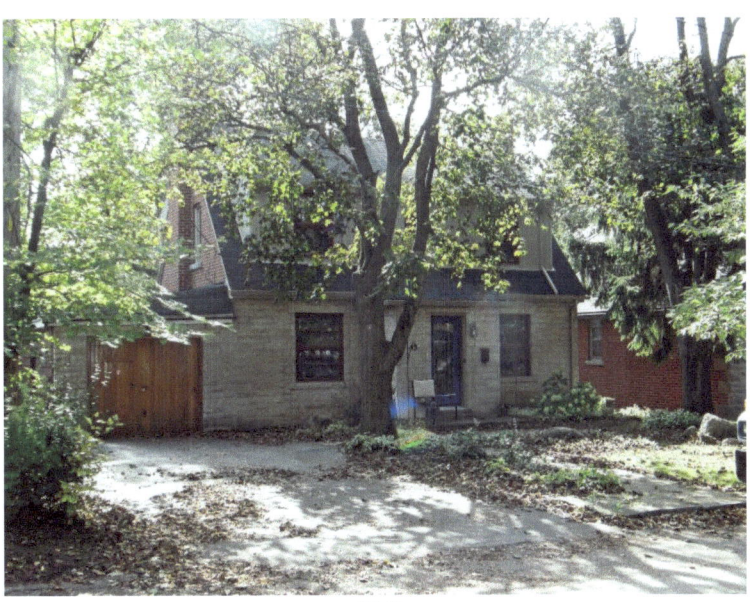

#13

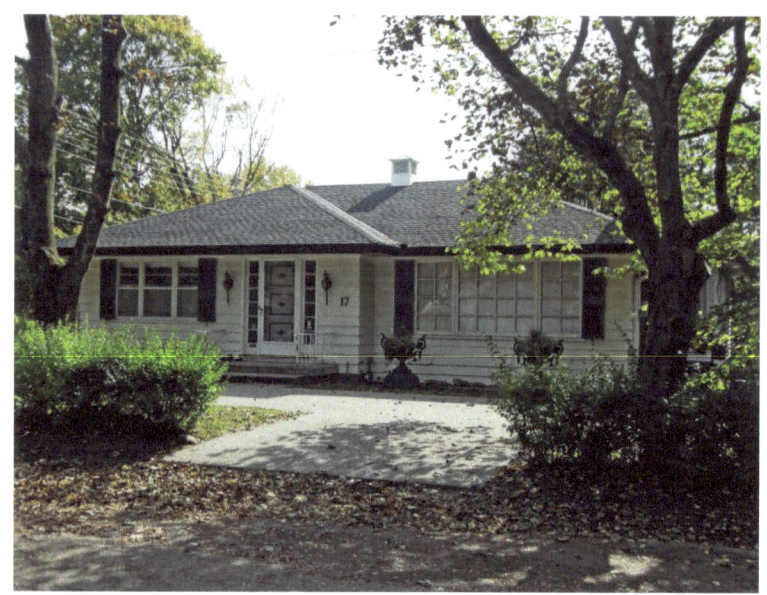

#17 - cottage

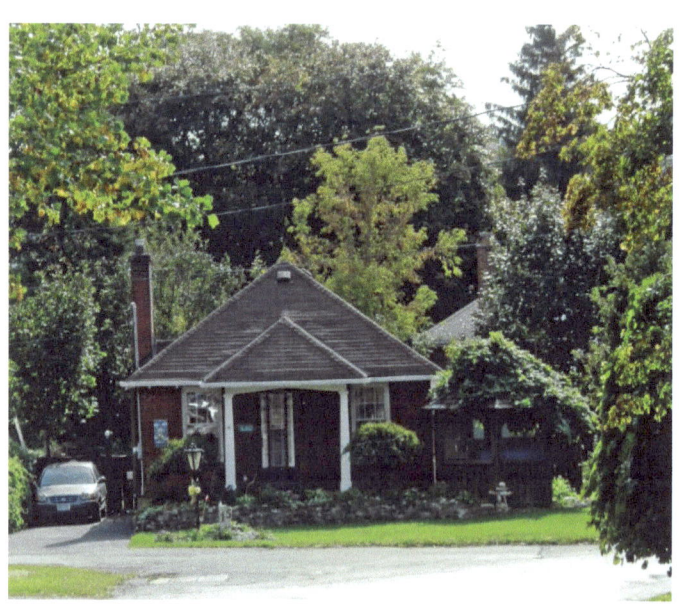

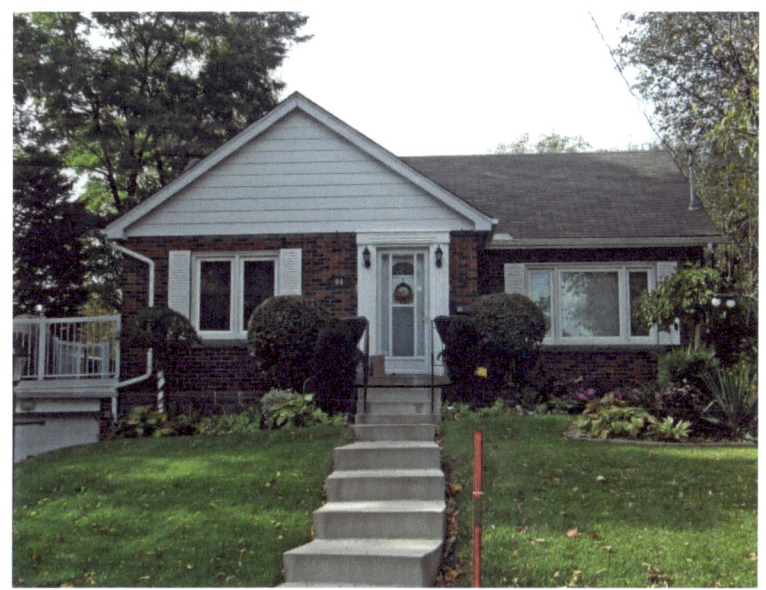

#64

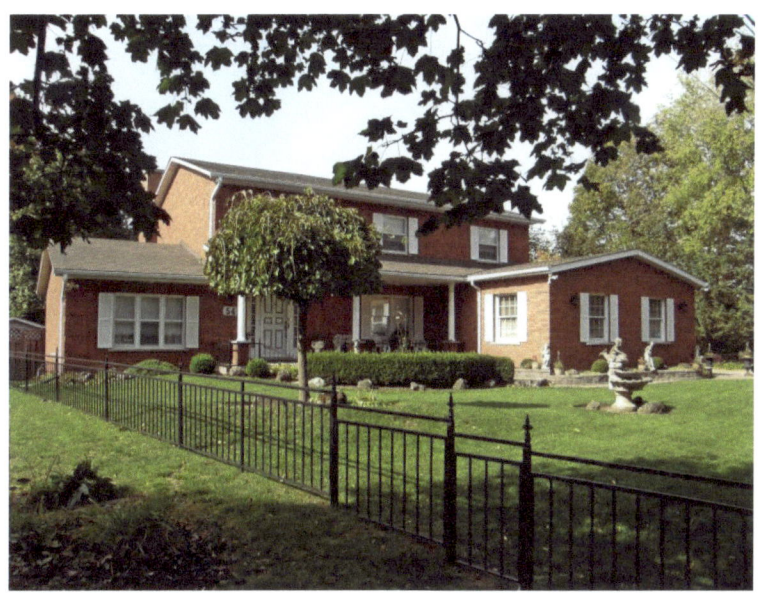

Valleyview 1978 - 54 East Street South

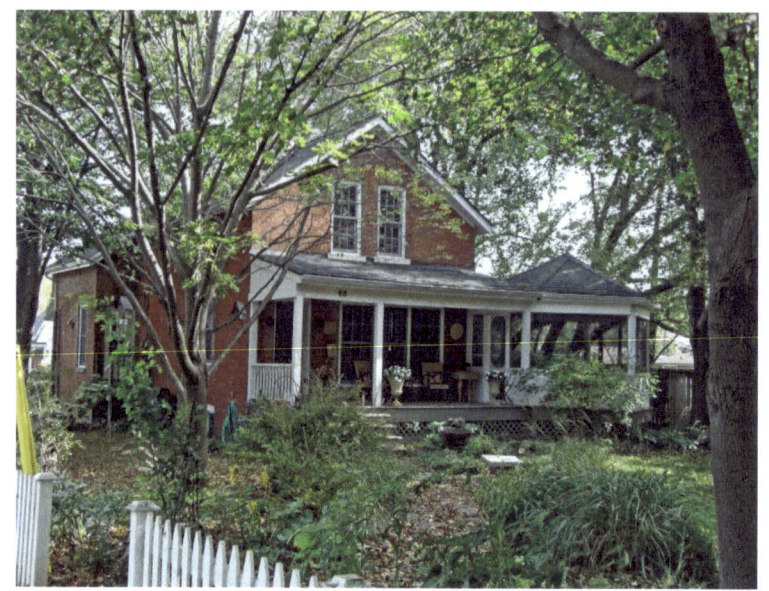

#69 Dunning Court

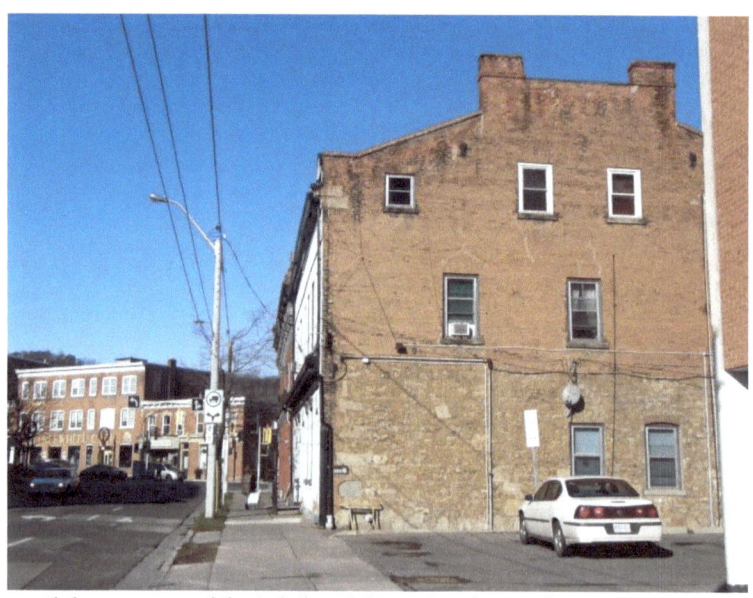

An old stone and brick building looking from Main Street
towards King Street

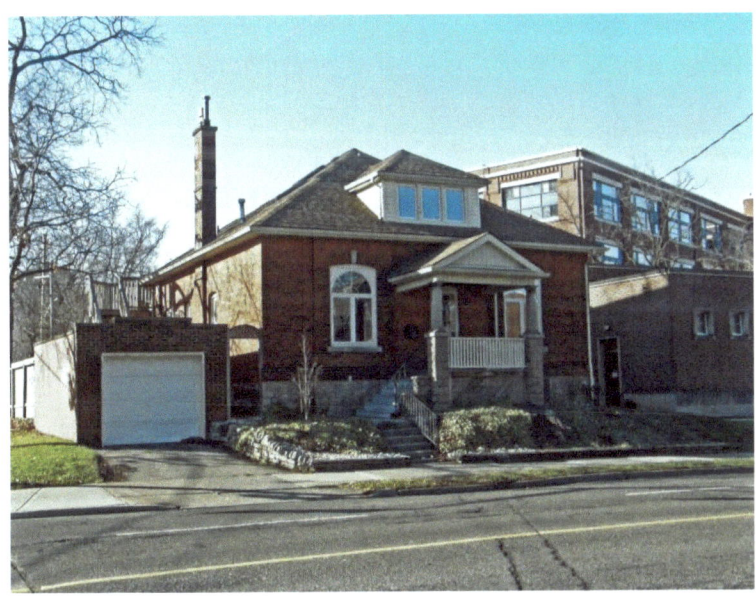

Main Street – Italianate – dormer in attic

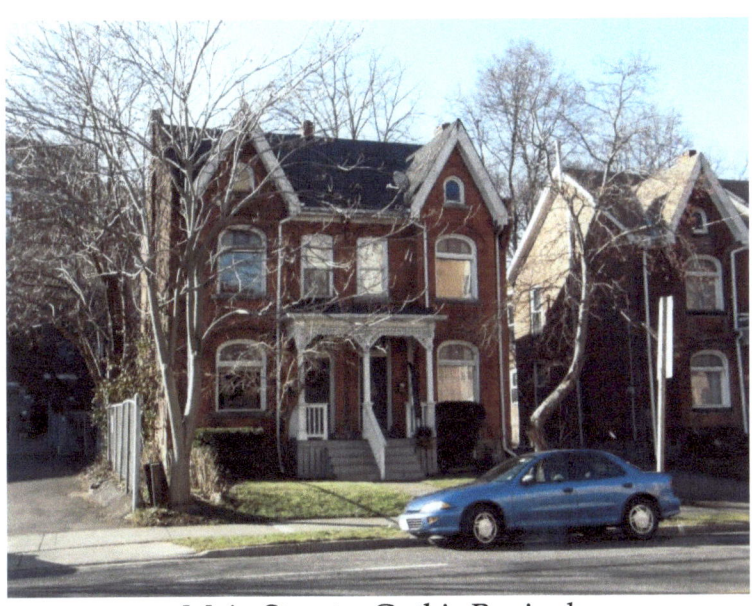

Main Street – Gothic Revival

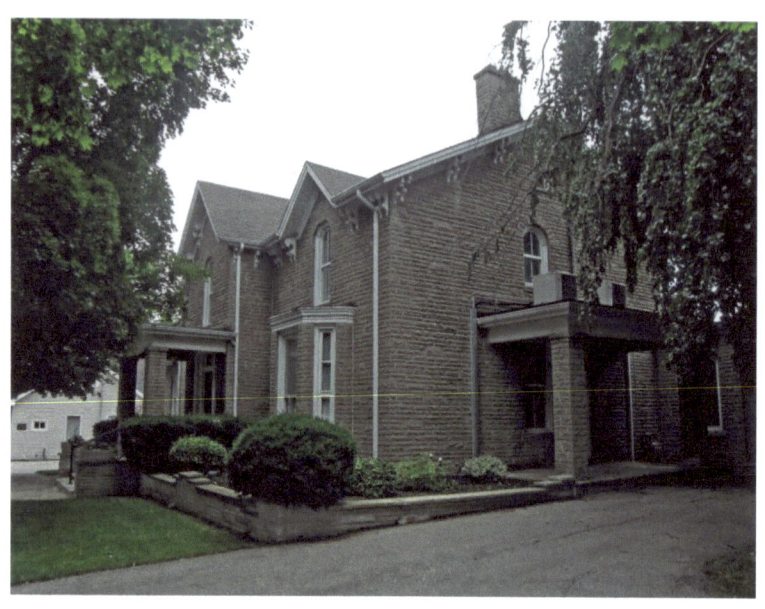

Cattel, Eaton and Chambers Funeral Home
53 Main Street

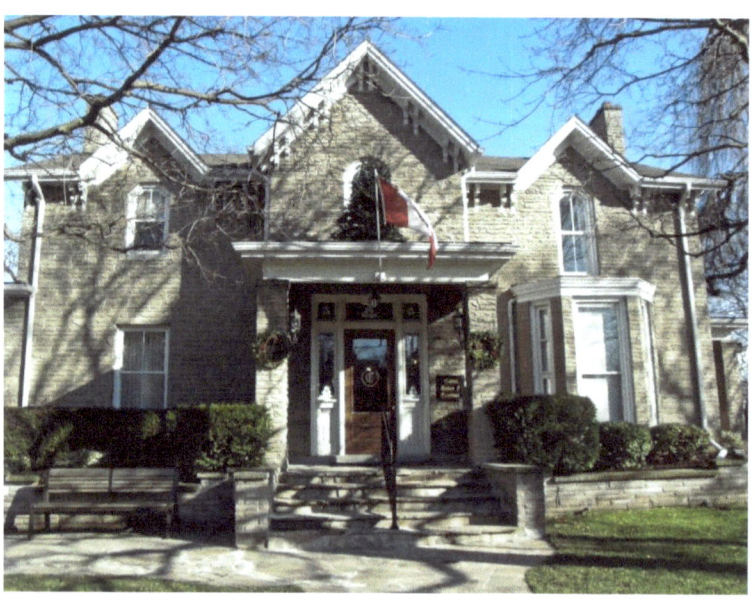

Gothic Revival – paired cornice brackets

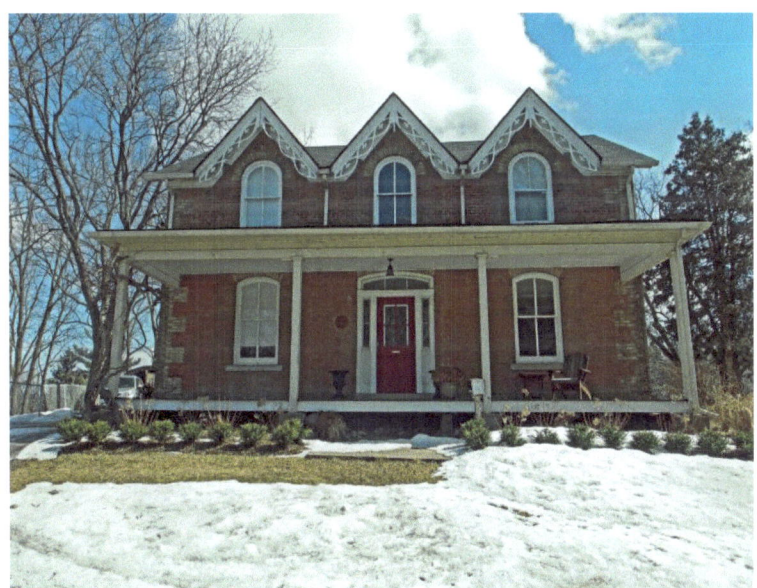

77 Creighton Road – Gothic Revival – Vergeboard trim, corner quoins

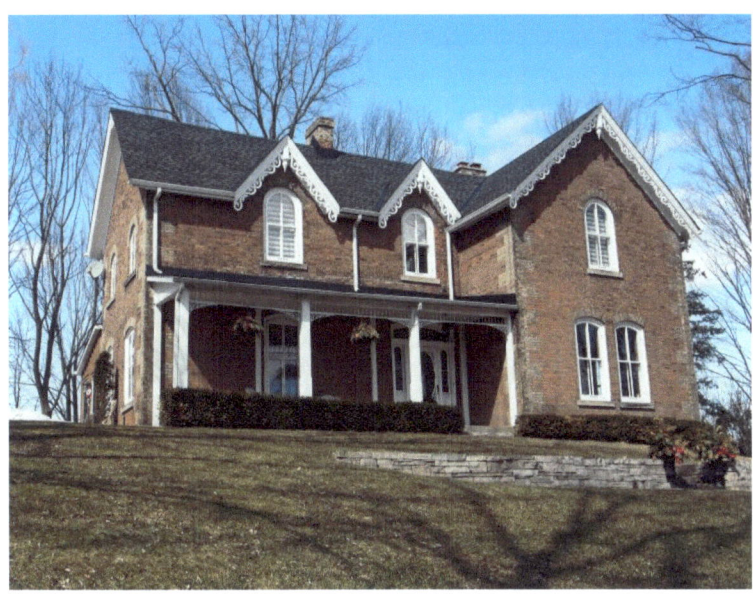

78 Creighton Road – Gothic Revival, Vergeboard trim, corner quoins, arched window voussoirs

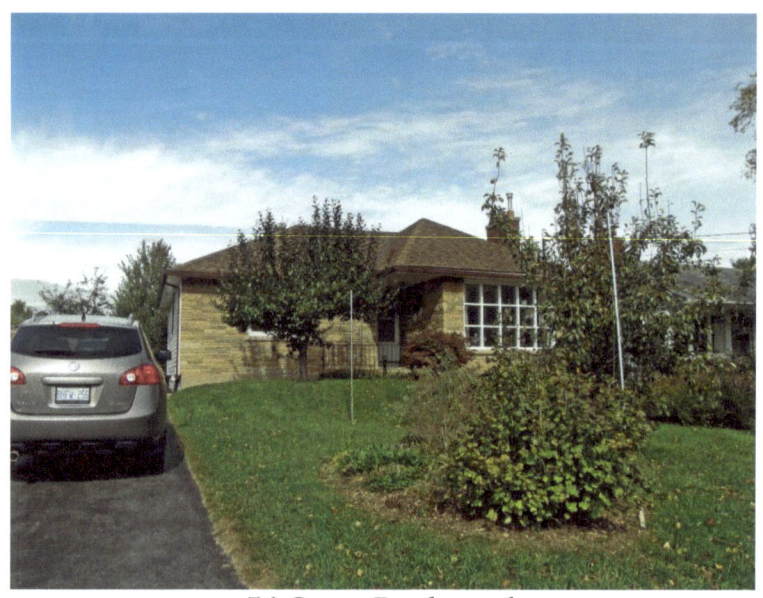

56 Grant Boulevard
Home of the Raues since August 2000
Built in 1953, one floor, three bedrooms, full basement

We added a vegetable garden in the backyard, raspberry, blueberry, black currant, red currant and gooseberry bushes, two pear trees and a cherry tree, as well as expanding the flower gardens.

Architectural Terms

Brackets: a decorative or weight-bearing structural element which forms a right angle with one side against a wall and the other under a projecting surface such as an eave or roof. Example: 53 Main Street	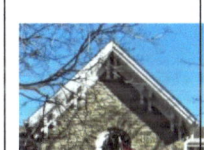
Belvedere: (from the Italian "beautiful view") an architectural feature on a roof, in a garden or on a terrace that gives a beautiful view. Example: South Street "Wedding Cake House"	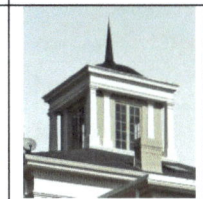
Cobblestone architecture: Refers to the use of cobblestones embedded in mortar as a method for erecting walls on houses and commercial buildings. Example: Cobblestone bridge at Webster's Falls	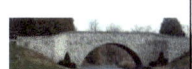
Cornice: originally the wooden overhang of the roof. With the use of stone, brick, iron and steel, the cornice is any projecting shelf at the top of a ceiling or roof. They can be very decorative. Example: 295 Brock Road	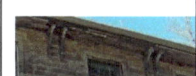
Cornice Return: decorative element on the end of a gable. Example: 667 Harvest Road	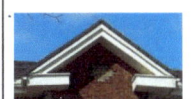
Dichromatic brickwork: the use of two colours of brick, tile or slate to decorate a façade. Example: 55 Sydenham Street	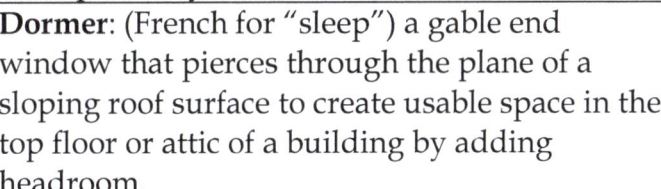
Dormer: (French for "sleep") a gable end window that pierces through the plane of a sloping roof surface to create usable space in the top floor or attic of a building by adding headroom. Example: 67 Sydenham Street	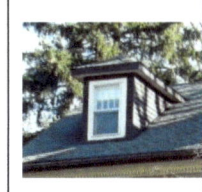

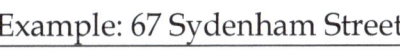

Finial: ornament added to the top of a gable, pinnacle, canopy or spire – a Gothic element. Example: 63-65 Sydenham Street	
Gable: the triangular portion of a wall between the edges of a sloping roof. Example: 64 South Street	
Hipped Roof: a roof where all sides slope downwards to the walls with no gables. Example: 24 South Street	
Keystones and Voussoirs: a voussoir is a wedge-shaped element used in building an arch. A keystone is the central stone that locks all the stones into position, allowing the arch to bear weight. A keystone is often enlarged and embellished. Example: 78 Creighton Road	
Palladian Window: a large window that is divided into three sections with the centre section larger than the two side sections and usually arched. Example: 82 Sydenham Street	
Pediment: a triangular section above the horizontal structure (entablature), typically supported by columns. The inside of the triangle is called the tympanum. Example: 60 Sydenham Street	
Vergeboards: also called bargeboards (gingerbread) – hang from the projecting end of a roof and are often elaborately carved and ornamented. Example: 77 Creighton Road	

Dundas's Building Styles

Edwardian, 1900-1930 – This style bridges the ornate and elaborate styles of the Victorian era and the simplified styles of the 20th century. Balanced facades, simple roof lines, dormer windows, large front porches, and smooth brick surfaces are its characteristics. Example: 82 Sydenham Street	
Georgian, before 1860 – This style began with the British King Georges in the 18th century. These buildings have balanced facades around a central door, medium-pitched gable roofs, and small paned windows. Example: 37 Cayley Street	
Gothic Revival, 1830-1890 – These decorative buildings have sharply-pitched gables with highly detailed vergeboards, pointed-arch window openings, and dichromatic brickwork. It is a common style in Ontario. Example: 63-65 Sydenham Street	
Italianate, 1850-1900 – It has wide-bracketed eaves, belvederes, wrap-around verandahs. Example: 71 and 73 Sydenham Street	
Regency Cottage, 1830-1860 – This style originated in England in 1815 and spread to Ontario later in the 19th century as British officers retired to Canada. It is a modest one-storey house with a low-pitched hip roof and has a symmetrical front façade. Example: Cayley Street	

www.ingramcontent.com/pod-product-compliance
Lightning Source LLC
Chambersburg PA
CBHW040840180526
45159CB00001B/250